Seattle
Cooks

JULIEN PERRY

Seattle Cooks

SIGNATURE RECIPES FROM THE CITY'S BEST CHEFS & BARTENDERS

Figure.1

Vancouver / Berkeley

Cataloguing data is available from Library and Archives Canada
ISBN 978-1-77327-035-7 (hbk.)

Design by Naomi MacDougall
Photography by Charity Burggraaf
Props and styling by Renée Beaudoin
Photo assistance by Audrey Kelly

Editing by Michelle Meade
Copy editing by Pam Robertson
Proofreading by Lucy Kenward
Indexing by Iva Cheung

Printed and bound in China by C&C Offset Printing Co., Ltd.
Distributed in the U.S. by Publishers Group West

Figure 1 Publishing Inc.
Vancouver BC Canada
www.figure1publishing.com

To cooks, aspiring cooks, and anyone who
loves good food and inspiring stories

Contents

Introduction

Seattle has changed dramatically in just a few short years. Some suggest that the city has finally evolved from a collection of homespun neighborhoods into a sophisticated enclave of high-end dining and luxury homes, while others bemoan encroaching biospheres and the collapse of rooftop water views. One thing is for certain: the foodscape has never been more robust.

How did it get that way? Let's look at what makes Seattle tick. You can't really describe the restaurant scene here without reference to what makes this city, well, a city. Much of Seattle's character has been shaped by the businesses that operate among us. We've collectively scooted over to make room for some notable multinational corporations—Microsoft, Boeing, Amazon, F5 Networks, Nintendo, Facebook, Apple, and Google—that have rebranded Seattle as a metropolis. And those same megacorps are creating well-paying jobs that, in turn, create an environment of consumers who can afford to dine out (among other things). And that is having a trickle-down effect on the food scene, most noticeably in terms of options. It's much easier for chefs to cook good food when the demand is high.

The chefs, bartenders, and bakers celebrated within the pages of this book are committed to making Seattle one of the best food cities in the country. At a time when foodie argot—"farm to table," "locally grown," and "organic"—has become a part of everyday vocabulary and "hippie food" is no longer pejorative, we have access to high-quality products that are being expressed on many levels, from food trucks to fast casual to fine dining. We consume some of the best seafood, wine, charcuterie, and foraged produce in the country without making a reservation, donning a tie, or, in the case of food delivery, putting on pants (metaphorically speaking). It's never been easier to get our hands on great food, even if those hands are busy ordering from an app.

As the city's population stretches to an almost uncomfortable girth, competition in the restaurant industry has swelled also. Entry level into the game now requires great technique and the best products. For a long time, Seattle cuisine mainly consisted of Thai, French, Mexican, and Italian. Now, we're seeing Malaysian, Latin American, and the cuisines of specific regions of Mexico. Because travel and information are more accessible than ever, chefs are able to explore and shift their interests. Fortunate is the Seattle diner who gets to reap these rewards.

For as much expansion as Seattle has undergone in a short amount of time, its restaurant community seems to be getting smaller by the day. While talking to the fine men and women featured in this book, I realized how intimate an industry it really is. Almost every participant is connected to another in some way; they're all intertwined, whether they worked together in the same kitchen at some point in their careers or gained tutelage from a shared mentor. *Seattle Cooks* is like the book version of a family tree, with recipes serving as the branches. Everyone in this book has learned from everyone else in this book. And now, you're about to learn from all of them.

If you're someone who's active in the local dining scene, many of these recipes will probably seem familiar. Not all are easy—you'll find techniques for every skill set—but all are meaningful in some way to the artisans who created them. *Seattle Cooks* is a collection of signature dishes, coveted recipes, original menu items, and tributes to restaurants we wish had never closed. Now, go out and support your neighborhood eateries—they're showcasing their best work!

The Restaurants

The Recipes

Mains

Sweets

Cocktails

Altura Nathan Lockwood

WHEN CURRENT trends lean toward casual concepts, Altura stands out for embracing its fine-dining focus. The Italian restaurant may not boast white linen table-cloths or hushed ambience (the music drifts from bluegrass to grunge on any given night), but it does offer something most other Seattle restaurants don't: a tasting menu that ranges from 12 to 18 courses. It's all part of chef-owner Nathan Lockwood's desire to surprise diners on a nightly basis and to introduce them to new and unexpected ingredients and flavors as they journey through the night's menu, which is only presented after the meal.

Lockwood opened Altura on Broadway in 2011 with a vision of partnering the skills he mastered while working for fine-dining superstars in San Francisco (including Hubert Keller and Suzette Gresham) with the bounty of produce, foraged goods, and spectacular seafood in the Northwest. The Short Rib Tortellini with bone marrow–roasted beets and fresh currants, finished with flowering fennel and house-grown dill, is one of Altura's most popular dishes; the incredibly earthy dish, with beautifully made pasta, truly speaks to Lockwood's modern Italian creativity.

Altura has proven that, despite outward appearances, Seattleites really do want to dine. Lockwood believes if you do it right, by putting as much focus on service and generosity as you do in making delicious food, people will respond by keeping your restaurant full.

PRESERVED LEMON AIOLI

3 egg yolks
2 cloves garlic
10 to 14 saffron threads
2 Tbsp chopped preserved
    lemon
1 Tbsp Dijon mustard
Zest and juice of 1 lemon
2 cups extra-virgin olive oil

MUSSELS

2 lbs live mussels, scrubbed
    and debearded
12 dried chiles de arbol
    or japones
12 cloves garlic, crushed
12 sprigs fresh Italian
    parsley
2 sprigs fresh thyme
2 Tbsp olive oil

12 thin slices pancetta or
    bacon (see Note)
Hardwood, such as
    madrone wood and bark,
    for smoking

Note: Altura uses their house-cured pancetta for wrapping the mussels, but you can find quality pancetta at your local butcher or deli counter. Be sure to have the pancetta sliced thinly—if the pancetta is too thick, it will overpower the mussels' delicate flavor.

Pancetta-Wrapped Mussels Grilled Over Madrone Wood

SERVES 2

Local seafood suppliers Salt Spring Island, Snow Creek, and Taylor Shellfish produce excellent Mediterranean-variety mussels—simply choose the largest, sweetest mussels you can find. During the fall and winter season, Altura serves a single large mussel under a dome of madrone bark smoke, which has a unique flavor profile of warm spice and citrus (although any hardwood smoke will do).

PRESERVED LEMON AIOLI In a blender, combine egg yolks, garlic, saffron, preserved lemon, mustard, lemon zest and juice. With the blender running, gradually add oil and blend until emulsified. Refrigerate while preparing the mussels.

MUSSELS Discard any mussels that are broken or do not shut when tapped. Put mussels into a large bowl, add chiles, garlic, parsley, thyme, and oil, and stir well. Heat a heavy-bottomed stockpot over high heat for 1 to 2 minutes, until very hot. Add mussel mixture, cover with a well-fitted lid, and cook 2 to 4 minutes, until mussels open. Discard any mussels that have not fully opened.

Reserving the cooking liquid, place the cooked mussels in a large dish or tray and spread out in a single layer. Cover loosely with plastic wrap or a kitchen towel and cool thoroughly. Once cool, remove the mussels from the shells, place them in a bowl, and strain the cooking liquid over them. Reserve mussels in the fridge and discard shells.

On a cutting board, lay a strip of pancetta lengthwise away from you. Place a mussel along the short edge and carefully roll it until the mussel is fully wrapped twice. Trim pancetta and use a skewer or toothpick to secure the loose end. Repeat with remaining mussels and set aside.

Preheat a grill with the wood and bark. Grill the mussels over the embers until crisp and heated through.

TO SERVE Transfer pancetta-wrapped mussels to a serving plate, and top each with preserved lemon aioli.

OXTAILS

5 lbs oxtails, cut into 2-inch-thick pieces and excess fat trimmed

Salt and freshly ground black pepper

¼ cup water

1 cup coarsely chopped carrots

1 cup coarsely chopped onions

1 cup coarsely chopped celery

1 cup coarsely chopped leeks

6 dried japones or chiles de arbol

3 sprigs fresh Italian parsley

3 sprigs fresh fennel fronds

1 fresh bay leaf

1 qt (4 cups) poultry stock, such as chicken, turkey, or duck

⅓ cup veal glace

TRIPE

2 lbs honeycomb tripe, scrubbed and rinsed

Salt and freshly ground black pepper

1 cup thinly sliced carrots

1 cup thinly sliced onions

1 cup thinly sliced celery

1 cup thinly sliced leeks

3 sprigs fresh Italian parsley

3 sprigs fresh fennel fronds

6 dried japones or chiles de arbol

Tripe and Oxtail Ragu with Pappardelle

SERVES 2 TO 4

Prepare the oxtails a day in advance. While the ragu is served with pappardelle at the restaurant, any pasta will work. Or try it with grilled bread, creamy polenta, or smashed potatoes—you won't be disappointed.

OXTAILS Lightly season oxtails with salt and pepper. Heat a large Dutch oven over medium to medium-high heat and brown the meat in a single layer (work in batches, if necessary, to avoid overcrowding). Transfer to a large plate after each batch.

Add water to deglaze the pot and add remaining ingredients. Bring to a boil and return oxtails to the pot. Add enough cold water to cover, bring back to a boil, and then simmer for 3 hours, or until just tender. Set aside to cool at room temperature for 1 hour.

Transfer oxtails to a clean pan. Strain the braising liquid over the oxtails and discard the aromatics and herbs. Set aside to cool, then refrigerate overnight.

TRIPE Lay a piece of tripe into a pot in which it just fits. Season with salt and pepper. Spread vegetables, herbs, and chiles evenly over the tripe. Repeat until all the tripe, vegetables, and herbs have been evenly layered. You should have at least three layers and all pieces of tripe should be separated by vegetables and aromatics.

Weigh down ingredients with a heavy weight (a clean Dutch oven filled with water works) and fill pot with enough water to just cover them. Bring to a boil, then reduce heat to medium-low, and gently simmer for 4 to 6 hours.

ASSEMBLY

4 cups peeled and chopped
  Roma tomatoes

1 clove garlic, finely grated

1 tsp Calabrian chili powder

1 tsp Korean chili flakes

¼ tsp cayenne pepper

2 tsp freshly ground
  black pepper

Salt, to taste

Cooked pappardelle,
  to serve

ASSEMBLY Remove oxtails from braising liquid and separate meat from bones. Slice tripe into 1-inch slices and reserve.

Strain oxtail and tripe braising liquids through a fine mesh strainer into a large saucepan and boil over high heat for 45 minutes to 1 hour, or until it is reduced by two-thirds (it might take longer depending on the size of your pan). The pan needs to be large enough to accommodate the reserved and portioned meats, chopped tomatoes, and finishing ingredients.

Add reserved oxtails, tripe, and chopped tomatoes to the reduced braising liquids and simmer over medium heat until thickened and warmed through. Add the garlic and spices and season to taste.

Barking Frog Bobby Moore

CHARISMA IS not a trait that can be learned or acquired—you simply have it or you don't. And chef Bobby Moore is someone who's got it . . . loads of it, which makes him the perfect host for the enthusiastic oenophiles in Washington's wine country. The exposed timber, concrete floors, and cozy communal fireplace of Barking Frog create a warm and inviting backdrop for a memorable dining experience. "We've never considered ourselves *not* a Seattle restaurant because I've never had the mentality that we're the only game in town, ever," says Moore. "We've always tried to be great."

Moore keeps pace with the daily demands of helming the kitchen at Willows Lodge (Woodinville's most popular getaway), which attracts winemakers, staycationers, and reality escapers. His refined comfort food offerings, including signature dishes such as buttermilk-brined chicken and braised pork belly, sit easily on the menu next to fresh seafood and delicate salads that speak to his love of seasonal colors and flavors. A classic heirloom tomato salad is gussied up with burrata and an intensely pink compressed watermelon. And in one of Moore's favorite dinner creations—the Dungeness crab—crabmeat is nearly upstaged by pickled peaches. (Fun fact: Moore is allergic to stone fruits.)

For a seasoned chef who worked his way up, back in the nineties, from busboy to sous chef at the beloved and departed Fullers, he still enjoys learning new tricks from his young crew. But it's his tenure in hospitality that aligns him with the restaurant's eponym—a nod to the Native American belief that a "barking" frog symbolizes abundance, harmony, and well-being. In his own way, so does Moore.

PICKLED PEACHES BRINE

3 cups rice vinegar
3 cups mirin
2 tsp green cardamom
1 Tbsp store-bought pickling spice
½ jalapeño pepper, halved lengthwise
4 ripe peaches, halved, stoned, and cut into 6 segments

LEMON AIOLI

1 egg
1 egg yolk
½ clove garlic
1 Tbsp freshly squeezed lemon juice
½ to ¾ cup grapeseed oil
Salt and ground white pepper, to taste

GREENS

⅓ cup Gewürztraminer vinegar
1½ Tbsp granulated sugar
1 cup grapeseed or canola oil
Salt and ground white pepper, to taste
4 cups watercress or mixed greens

ASSEMBLY

1 lb cooked Dungeness crabmeat, shredded
⅓ cup lemon aioli (see here)
3 pinches celery seeds
Salt and freshly ground black pepper, to taste

Dungeness Crab and Pickled Peach Salad

SERVES 4

PICKLED PEACHES BRINE Combine vinegar, mirin, cardamom, pickling spice, and jalapeño pepper in a medium saucepan and bring to a boil over medium-high heat. Strain liquid to remove the spices and set aside to cool.

In a large bowl or container, combine the peaches and the cooled brine, cover, and pickle overnight in the fridge.

LEMON AIOLI Place egg, egg yolk, garlic, and lemon juice in food processor. With the food processor running, gradually add oil and blend until emulsified. Season with salt and pepper to taste.

GREENS Combine vinegar and sugar in a blender and pulse to blend. With the blender running, gradually add oil and blend until emulsified. Season with salt and pepper.

Put watercress or greens into a large bowl, add 2 tablespoons vinaigrette, and toss. (The remaining vinaigrette can be stored in the fridge for up to three weeks.)

ASSEMBLY Toss the crabmeat, lemon aioli, and celery seeds thoroughly in a small bowl, and season to taste. Plate a quarter of the mixture using a ring mold, and top with greens. Arrange 3 to 4 pickled peach slices around the salad. Repeat with the remaining plates.

ROASTED TOMATO SALSA

1 yellow onion, coarsely chopped

1 poblano chile, seeded and chopped

2 ancho chiles, seeded

4 tomatoes, seeded and coarsely chopped

1 bunch fresh cilantro (about 4 cups)

Salt and freshly ground black pepper, to taste

CHORIZO HASH

1 Tbsp canola or grapeseed oil

½ yellow onion, chopped

2 lbs Mexican chorizo

½ red bell pepper, seeded and chopped

RANCH BEANS

1 Tbsp canola or grapeseed oil

½ onion, coarsely chopped

½ poblano chile, seeded and coarsely chopped

½ red bell pepper, seeded and coarsely chopped

2 cloves garlic, finely chopped

2 (15-oz) cans black beans, drained

1 cup water

2 tsp ground cumin

2 tsp ancho chili powder

1 tsp salt

ASSEMBLY

2 Tbsp vegetable oil

8 to 12 farm-fresh eggs

8 to 12 tostada shells

½ cup shredded cheddar

3 Tbsp roasted tomato salsa (see here)

1 Tbsp sour cream

¼ cup chopped fresh cilantro

Half an avocado, sliced (optional)

Crumbled cotija cheese, for garnish (optional)

Huevos Rancheros

SERVES 4 TO 6

ROASTED TOMATO SALSA Preheat oven to 425°F.

Put onion, chiles, and tomatoes on a baking sheet, toss, and roast for 15 to 20 minutes, or until the edges darken. Set aside to cool.

Transfer mixture to a blender, add cilantro, and pulse until puréed. Season with salt and pepper. (Leftover salsa can be stored in the fridge for up to 4 days.)

CHORIZO HASH Heat oil in a skillet over medium-high heat, add onion, and sauté for 7 minutes, until translucent. Add chorizo and sauté for another 5 minutes, breaking it up with a wooden spoon. Add bell pepper and sauté for 3 minutes, until it is tender.

RANCH BEANS Heat oil in a saucepan over medium heat. Add onion, chile, and bell pepper and sauté for 7 minutes until softened. Add garlic and cook for 1 to 2 minutes. Stir in beans, water, cumin, chili powder, and salt.

Insert an immersion blender into the pan and, keeping it still, blend some of the bean mixture. You want to blend a small portion of the beans to help give them a creamy texture. (Alternatively, transfer some of the beans into a blender and purée.)

ASSEMBLY Heat 1 tablespoon oil in a large nonstick pan over medium heat. Crack in half the eggs and fry for 3 to 5 minutes, until whites are set on top and yolks are still runny. Using a spatula, slide an egg on top of each tostada shell. Repeat with the remaining oil and eggs.

Put ranch beans onto the plates and top with tostadas and eggs, then chorizo hash. Top with cheddar. Garnish with roasted tomato salsa. Finish with a dollop of sour cream, cilantro, sliced avocado, and cotija cheese, if using. Serve.

Barrio Casey Robison

CASEY ROBISON'S name is synonymous with mezcal in Seattle. He is the beverage director of the Heavy Restaurant Group, and has been with the company since 2008—he was initially hired to be the opening bar manager of Barrio, a spirits sanctum with altar-like walls of flickering candles and a wooden entry door heavy enough to abolish every sin.

Just five years prior, Robison was getting his (barely legal) feet wet barbacking at the now-defunct B&O Espresso café. Then it was on to more notable spots like Chez Gaudy and Café Presse, where he introduced cocktail enthusiasts to the gin-and-absinthe-based Corpse Reviver in 2006. But something really sparked in him when he helped open The Saint on Capitol Hill, where he would learn all about tequila and find his niche in mezcal.

Barrio is the perfect spot for Robison to spread the gospel of mezcal—he's stocked the bar with 164 labels (and counting), making it the second largest selection in the country. Brace yourself: he's not the biggest cocktail enthusiast. While he loves the action and social aspect of bartending, for him, spirits provide a voyeuristic view into different cultures. And because Robison is a big traveler, nothing satiates him more than unearthing new discoveries and drinking in their crazy backstories; it's more about the intellectual curiosity of spirits than it is about the bottle in front of him.

→ El Nacional (front) and Wolverine Blues

1 oz Del Maguey
  Vida mezcal
1 oz Campari
½ oz Luxardo Amaro Abano
½ oz Yzaguirre Reserva dry
  vermouth
2 dashes Scrappy's
  chocolate bitters
3 drops Ardbeg 10-Year-Old
  Islay scotch
Lemon peel, for garnish

El Nacional

SERVES 1

This drink came into creation around 2010 when a colorful patron asked Casey Robison to make him something similar to kissing a fist fight. "I loved how that sounded! Mezcal, different amari, scotch, and dry vermouth sounded about right," says Robison. "While the drink has been on and off the menu ever since, it is still one of my favorites to serve."

Combine mezcal, Campari, Amaro Abano, vermouth, and bitters in a mixing glass with ice. Stir and strain into a chilled coupe or cocktail glass. Add scotch and garnish with lemon peel.

1½ oz Suntory Toki
   Japanese whisky
½ oz Manzanilla sherry
¾ oz Giffard Banane
   du Brésil liqueur
¼ oz Cynar
Lemon peel, for garnish

Wolverine Blues

SERVES 1

"This cocktail is named after a record by a Swedish death metal band called Entombed," says Robison. "When I was a barback at Clever Dunne's, the bartender Fernando always played the record while we closed the bar. Years later, I thought it would be the coolest name for a cocktail."

Combine liquid ingredients in a mixing glass with ice. Stir. Strain into an old-fashioned glass over a large ice cube and garnish with a twist of lemon peel.

Brimmer & Heeltap Mike Whisenhunt

WHEN IT was announced in 2013 that chef Mike Whisenhunt would be helping to transform the old Le Gourmand space with proprietor Jen Doak, you could almost hear a collective proclamation of "They have big shoes to fill!" over Seattle. But with Doak's inherent knack of working a dining room (nobody is more personable) and Whisenhunt's playful menu, this gastropub met every expectation.

Whisenhunt's boldly flavored dishes are approachable but complex enough that the average home-cook wouldn't attempt to duplicate them. We're talking Fresno chile hot sauces fermented with *koji* (a fungus most commonly used to ferment soybeans), steak tartare with soy-cured egg yolk, and grilled pork shoulder with fermented chickpeas, chiles, and pickled Fuji apples. Many of his wild flavor combinations were born from his time working with Rachel Yang and Seif Chirchi at Revel (page 138). "They were unique, different, and inspiring at a time when I needed it," says Whisenhunt, crediting Yang for bringing fusion back and influencing his cooking style, such as by adding a "wow" factor to a familiar dish.

The farmhouse chic interior—with wood tables and teal cushion and lighting accents—is simple and elegant, and made memorable with a penny-covered floor in the back room (which required more than 75,000 coins to create). It's a gentle reflection of Whisenhunt's preference for preparing recognizable dishes with unexpected flavor components. He and Doak have filled the big shoes and then some.

→ Roasted Cauliflower Salad

FERMENTED GARLIC

3 Tbsp salt

4 cups warm water

2 heads garlic, cloves separated and peeled

FERMENTED GARLIC VINAIGRETTE

5 cloves fermented garlic (see here)

½ cup fermented garlic liquid (see here)

½ cup rice wine vinegar

1 Tbsp dry mustard

1 Tbsp salt

2 cups grapeseed oil

PICKLED MUSHROOMS

4 cups rice vinegar

4 cups granulated sugar

1 lb assorted mushrooms, such as chanterelles and black trumpets, cleaned

QUINOA

¼ cup black quinoa

½ cup water

1 (½-inch) piece ginger, peeled

Salt, to taste

ROASTED CAULIFLOWER

2 heads cauliflower, separated into 1-inch florets

2 to 3 Tbsp olive oil

Salt, to taste

SALAD

5 to 6 cups loosely packed arugula

2 Tbsp fermented garlic vinaigrette (see here)

Salt and freshly ground black pepper, to taste

Roasted Cauliflower Salad

SERVES 4 TO 6

The key to this signature menu item is fermented garlic. You only need a couple of cloves for the recipe, but it is better to prepare a whole lot of them so you always have them on hand. Leftover vinaigrette can be stored in an airtight container in the fridge for up to a month.

FERMENTED GARLIC Combine salt and water in a large bowl and stir.

Place garlic in a large sterilized jar and add enough of the saltwater solution to cover the garlic. Cover jar with a breathable linen and wrap string around it to keep it secured. Store jar in a location that is 55°F to 65°F and allow to ferment for three days to three weeks, until the garlic is translucent and the liquid is creamy when stirred. It can be stored in the fridge for up to six months.

FERMENTED GARLIC VINAIGRETTE In a blender, combine fermented garlic, garlic liquid, vinegar, mustard, and salt and blend on high until smooth. With the blender running, gradually add oil and blend until emulsified. Pour into a squeeze bottle and chill.

PICKLED MUSHROOMS Bring vinegar to a boil in a large saucepan. Add sugar, stir, and bring to a boil again.

Put mushrooms into a heatproof bowl and pour in the vinegar mixture. Allow to cool, cover with a lid, and refrigerate until use.

QUINOA Put quinoa, water, and ginger into a large saucepan and bring to a boil over high heat. Reduce to medium-low heat, season with salt, and simmer for 15 to 20 minutes, until cooked through and liquid has been absorbed. Transfer to a shallow container and chill until needed.

Note: Be sure vinaigrette is creamy, otherwise, remake it. To help stabilize the vinaigrette, you can add small amounts of xanthan gum, which is available at most grocery stores. Store in a squeeze bottle or jar and shake before use.

ROASTED CAULIFLOWER Preheat oven to 500°F. Line a baking sheet with parchment paper.

Place florets on the prepared baking sheet and drizzle with enough oil to lightly coat. Lightly season with salt, toss, and spread florets out in a single layer. Roast for 20 minutes, until browned. (Don't worry if some look a little too dark. Check after 10 minutes and remove any that are ready.) Set aside to cool, then chill in fridge.

SALAD In a large bowl, combine cauliflower, quinoa, arugula and pickled mushrooms (drained, brine discarded). Drizzle with fermented garlic vinaigrette and toss. Add more to taste, if necessary. Adjust salt and pepper to taste. Be careful not to overseason or overdress.

Transfer to a serving platter and serve.

SEASONING SAUCE

½ cup sake

½ cup mirin

2 Tbsp freshly squeezed lime juice

2 Tbsp grated ginger

2 Tbsp fish sauce (Three Crabs brand preferred)

FRIED RICE

2 Tbsp canola oil

1 cup cooked short-grain brown rice, chilled

¼ poblano chile, seeded and thinly sliced

¼ yellow onion, thinly sliced

3½ oz squid tubes and tentacles, drained well and sliced into ¼-inch rings

¼ cup seasoning sauce (see here)

¾ cup fresh Thai basil, thinly sliced (divided)

Salt, to taste

Red pepper flakes, to taste

Lime wedges, to serve

Note: The seasoning sauce can be stored in the fridge for up to two months. When ready to use, add an extra squeeze of lime juice.

Squid Fried Rice

SERVES 1

Making this dish in small batches is important to ensure that everything sears in the pan. If you want to double this recipe, you'll basically need to make it twice.

SEASONING SAUCE Combine ingredients in a blender and process until smooth. Refrigerate until needed.

FRIED RICE Heat a large wok or large skillet over high heat until slightly smoking. Add oil and tilt pan to coat. Working quickly, add rice and sauté for 10 to 20 seconds, until lightly toasted. Add chile and onion and sauté for another 20 to 30 seconds, until they sizzle. Add squid and cook for another 20 seconds. Pour in seasoning sauce, stir well, and cook until rice has absorbed all the sauce. Fold in ½ cup of the Thai basil and season with salt and red pepper flakes. Transfer to a bowl or serving platter and garnish with the remaining Thai basil. Serve with lime wedges.

ChefSteps Grant Crilly

SEATTLE NATIVE Grant Crilly was one of those kids who took apart electronics and other machinery to see how things worked. Back then it was cute. Now, it's defined his career.

Crilly cooked in France and India and spent time at the original Mistral before spending a solid five years at the ultimate food lab—Modernist Cuisine—where he met Chris Young and Ryan Matthew Smith. By 2012, they launched ChefSteps, a food and technology company that aims to help people cook smarter.

The space—an unassuming office, several floors beneath the fish and produce stands of Pike Place Market—has been around for ages. But today, some of the most innovative cooking techniques are being tested there, to help the company move toward its goal of creating a future that enables home-cooks to shine. They've developed a sleek home sous-vide device called Joule, which manages heat, time, and temperature—variables that even the most skilled

chefs can struggle with. At a time when consumers want their food *right now*, ChefSteps inspires and empowers home-cooks to create their own dining experiences—without the help of a delivery driver.

Crilly uses food as a relationship builder, whether it's cooking for people or showing them how to turn ingredients into food. As a sexier, smarter, and more entertaining version of *America's Test Kitchen*, ChefSteps also offers online video tutorials that are geared to a generation that grew up watching the Food Network and now has a great appreciation for cooking. He's banking on a future in which people use food the same way he does—to bond and have fun while not overthinking things. His advice? Just chill out and cook already.

→ Char Siu

4 lbs pork collar or
  shoulder, cut into
  1½-inch-thick steaks

2 Tbsp salt

1 cup Lee Kum Kee Char
  Siu Sauce

1 cup Chinese hot mustard,
  to serve

½ cup sesame seeds,
  to serve

2 bunches scallions,
  sliced, to serve

Char Siu
(Cantonese-Style BBQ Pork)

SERVES 4 TO 6

To make this dish, you'll need a sous-vide cooker, a grill or broiler, some pork collar (or shoulder), and a half day of patience. The chefs at ChefSteps create their own marinades, but the results with Lee Kum Kee Char Siu Sauce (available at Asian supermarkets or online) are just as tasty. Keep a jar of that delicious condiment on hand, and you'll have a foolproof dish that requires very little effort.

Set up a sous-vide cooker in a large pot with enough water to cover the meat and set to 140°F. Place each steak in a separate large, heavy-duty ziplock bag, add char siu sauce and salt, and carefully lower into the pot. Set a timer for at least 8 hours (and up to 24 hours for extremely tender pork).

Transfer pork to a plate. Pour sauce into a saucepan and bring to a boil over medium-high heat. Reduce heat to medium-low and simmer for 15 minutes, until sauce is reduced and the texture resembles a thick honey.

Preheat grill (or broiler) to high heat. Add pork and grill (or broil) for 5 minutes, flipping frequently and brushing with glaze, until charred and dark. Transfer pork to a cutting board, slice thinly, and serve with hot mustard, sesame seeds, and scallions.

6 oz dark chocolate,
70% cacao, roughly
chopped
3 eggs
¾ cup heavy cream
¾ cup half-and-half cream
½ cup granulated sugar
1 tsp vanilla extract
½ tsp salt

Candied nuts, crushed,
for garnish
Fresh berries, for garnish

Bittersweet Chocolate Semifreddo

SERVES 8

This soft, semi-frozen mousse is easy to prepare with minimal effort but requires a bit of advance planning. You'll need a couple tools but that's part of the fun!

Using a sous-vide cooker, heat a large pot of water to 149°F. (Alternatively, warm a large pot of water on the stove and hold heat at 149°F, but it's tricky to maintain.)

Combine ingredients (except for the garnishes) in a bowl, then pour into a ziplock bag. Place into a water bath for 1 hour and agitate bag a couple of times to ensure even cooking. Remove the ziplock bag and strain into a metal bowl. Place the bowl into another bowl filled with ice to cool down. Place in the fridge and chill until mixture is 40°F.

Pour the chocolate mixture into a whip cream canister and charge with 3 nitrous charges.

Line a standard loaf pan with plastic wrap, then fill pan with chocolate mousse. Working quickly, use a palette knife or offset spatula to smooth out the top, then cover with plastic wrap and place in the freezer overnight.

To serve, unmold semifreddo onto a cutting board. Dip a sharp knife into hot water and dry with a kitchen towel, then use it to cut semifreddo into ½-inch slices. Plate and garnish with crushed candied nuts and fresh berries.

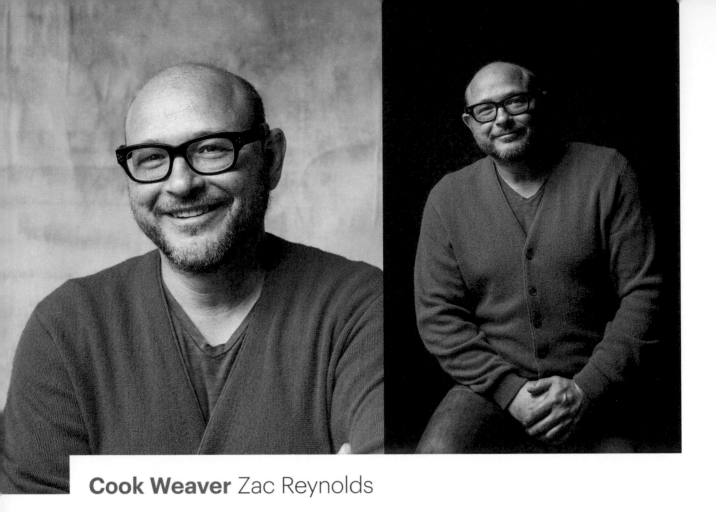

Cook Weaver Zac Reynolds

RESTAURANT PARTNERSHIPS come in many forms: sometimes they're forged by good friends, a big chunk of investor money, or in the case of Zac Reynolds, Craigslist. Anxious to find a partner to help him open a restaurant, he placed an ad and received a quick response from one Nile Klein—a veteran of Umi Sake House and Kushibar—who was also looking for a new project. The two found a home in the historic Loveless Building, an enchanting little neighborhood spot that has seen a revolving roster of great restaurants like Olivar and Restaurant Marron.

Adorning the walls of the space is a giant mural of Alexander Pushkin's "The Tale of Tsar Saltan," a poem about a tsar who chooses the youngest of three sisters to be his wife, while the other two are delegated to serving as cook and weaver. (The inspiration behind the restaurant name.) In anticipation of Cook Weaver, Reynolds worked as a private chef and hosted a string of pop-ups at Cortona Cafe in the Central District so he could test recipes and get a feel for his cuisine. His menus are created on a whim, depending on what sparks his interest—a typical week will likely see the collision of several cultures, with items such as Korean-inspired beer-battered nori dumplings with kimchi, salmon pastrami lettuce wraps with sauerkraut salad, and a Vietnamese crepe stuffed with greens. Reynolds's fun, exciting, and bold food speaks to his playful and relaxed attitude.

Oh, and there's also the communal chef's table in the farmhouse-inspired kitchen, which allows Reynolds to banter with his guests while he's cooking. Meanwhile, his equally affable counterpart Klein tends to the cozy five-seat bar—a welcome addition to the surrounding tableaus. It's the neighborhood dinner party of your dreams.

→ King Oyster Mushrooms with Pea Spaetzle

1 cup (2 sticks) plus 1 Tbsp cold unsalted butter, cubed (divided)

3 Tbsp finely chopped shallots

10 sprigs fresh thyme

¼ cup apple cider vinegar

¼ cup heavy cream

Salt, to taste

Shaved Parmesan, to serve

1 lb king oyster mushrooms, halved, or whole button mushrooms

¼ cup (½ stick) unsalted butter

¼ cup fermented black beans in oil (available at most Asian grocers)

King Oyster Mushrooms with Pea Spaetzle

SERVES 2

This dish mixes different cultural notes. Chef Zac Reynolds stocks a lot of Asian condiments and sauces in order to create big, boldly flavored dishes without necessarily making them "Asian." This is an impressive dish to serve to family and friends, but Reynolds tells us the pasta is equally delicious on its own with butter, peas, and grated Parmesan.

BEURRE BLANC Heat 1 tablespoon butter in a small saucepan over medium-high heat, add shallots and thyme, and sauté for 4 minutes, until shallots are translucent. Add vinegar and simmer for 10 minutes, until almost completely evaporated. Add cream and simmer, until reduced by two-thirds. Remove pan from heat and add ¼ cup (½ stick) chilled butter, gently stirring until melted. Add remaining butter, ¼ cup at a time, until used. Strain, season with salt, and set aside.

KING OYSTER MUSHROOMS Preheat oven to 450°F.

Using a small knife, score a crosshatch pattern into the mushrooms. Melt butter in a large cast-iron skillet over medium-high heat. Place mushrooms cut side down in the pan, working in batches if necessary, and brown. (If working in batches, divide butter accordingly.) Transfer mushrooms to a plate as they brown.

Return mushrooms to the skillet, add black bean sauce, and toss to coat. Transfer to a baking sheet and roast for 5 minutes. Set aside.

PEA SPAETZLE
3 cups frozen peas, thawed
3 egg yolks
1⅓ cups tapioca starch
¾ cup all-purpose flour
2 Tbsp salt

PEA SPAETZLE Combine peas and yolks in a high-power blender (such as a Vitamix) and blend until smooth. (If using a standard blender, add 1 tablespoon water to help loosen the mixture.) Scrape purée into a bowl, add remaining ingredients, and mix well.

Bring a large pot of water to a boil. Working in batches, transfer mixture to a spaetzle pasta maker and press into the pot. (Alternatively, use a silicone spatula to press batter through the large holes of a flat grater.) Cook for 1 to 2 minutes, until spaetzle floats to the surface. Using a slotted spoon, transfer the pasta to a bowl. Add a pinch of salt.

PLATING Distribute the spaetzle into bowls, lay mushrooms on top in a crisscross pattern, and spoon over beurre blanc to one side of the spaetzle. Scatter Parmesan on top and serve.

SUNFLOWER FINANCIERS

½ cup (1 stick) unsalted butter

1 cup raw sunflower seeds

½ cup all-purpose flour

1 tsp salt

1 tsp baking powder

4 egg whites

½ cup loosely packed brown sugar

½ cup granulated sugar, plus extra for dusting

RED WINE–CHERRY COMPOTE

1½ lbs Bing cherries, pitted

½ bottle good-quality red wine (we prefer Pinot)

¾ cup granulated sugar

4 star anise

Gooey Caramel Cake

SERVES 5

Prepare this dessert when Bing cherries are in season and use a Pinot or good-quality red wine for maximum flavor.

SUNFLOWER FINANCIERS Preheat oven to 425°F. Grease five (10-ounce) cocottes (see Note) or ramekins and dust with sugar.

Melt butter in a small, heavy-bottomed saucepan over medium-low heat and cook for 3 to 5 minutes, until nutty and dark brown. (This is called beurre noir or black butter.) Transfer to a small bowl, scraping all the burnt bits (milk solids) from the bottom of the pot. Set aside until cooled to room temperature.

Put sunflower seeds into a food processor and grind until there's a coarse, flour-like consistency. Add flour, salt, and baking powder, mix well, and set aside.

In a large mixing bowl, combine egg whites and sugars and stir vigorously until smooth. Add the flour mixture to the egg mixture and combine until smooth. Whisk in melted butter. (Be sure the butter is cooled down, otherwise the cakes will break.)

Place cocottes on a baking sheet. Scoop ½ cup of batter into each cocotte. Bake for 20 to 25 minutes until golden brown, rotate baking sheet halfway through (if not using a convection oven). Remove from oven and invert cakes onto a cooling rack. Set aside. (The cakes can be prepared up to two days in advance and stored in an airtight container.) Rinse cocottes.

RED WINE–CHERRY COMPOTE Combine ingredients in a saucepan and simmer over medium heat for 30 minutes, until reduced to ½ cup. Remove star anise, then refrigerate. (The compote can be made up to a week in advance and refrigerated.)

NUTELLA CARAMEL

1 cup granulated sugar
½ cup water
¾ cup heavy cream
¼ cup (½ stick) unsalted butter
¼ cup Nutella
1 tsp salt

CREAM CHEESE ICING

1 cup cream cheese
3 Tbsp granulated sugar
Zest of ½ lemon

Note: Cocottes are cast-iron pots used to serve soup or cook individual corn breads. They can be substituted with 4-inch ramekins or a heavy-duty muffin pan. The cooking time may need to be adjusted slightly.

NUTELLA CARAMEL Combine sugar and water in a heavy-bottomed saucepan and cook over medium heat for 10 minutes, or until dark brown. (Or until the temperature on a candy thermometer reaches 375°F to 380°F.) The bitterness of the caramel will cut through some of the sweetness of the dish.

Remove from heat and add remaining ingredients, stirring with a heatproof spatula or wooden spoon to prevent it from bubbling up. Set aside. (The caramel can be made up to a week in advance.)

CREAM CHEESE ICING In a stand mixer fitted with a paddle attachment, combine ingredients and mix until softened.

PLATING Preheat oven to 475°F.

Put 1 tablespoon Nutella caramel into the bottom of each cocotte and place cakes into each cocotte. Pour 3 tablespoons caramel over each cake, making sure to cover all sides. (Add more caramel if necessary.) Put cocottes onto a baking sheet and bake for 15 minutes, or until the caramel starts to bubble and the cakes are heated through.

Splatter a generous amount of red wine–cherry compote onto each plate, then smear a large tablespoon of cream cheese icing through the sauce. (The plates should look messy, like a Jackson Pollock painting!) Turn the cakes out onto the baking sheet. Using an offset spatula, place each cake on a plate and serve.

Copine Shaun McCrain

THERE IS no other Seattle restaurant quite like Copine. While it has the finesse of a fine-dining restaurant, it remains accessible, with a warm, neighborhood feel. Chef-owner Shaun McCrain works hard to ensure each little component of a plate—whether it's texture or flavor—adds something to the whole, and his consistency and attention to laser-precise detail result in refined, beautifully executed food. One dish that springs to mind is his Beef Tartare, prepared with marbled American Wagyu beef and elevated with seasonal accompaniments such as spring vegetables and *gribiche* (an egg dressing) or black truffle *aigre-doux* and russet potato chips.

McCrain spent years working at multi-Michelin-starred restaurants in Paris, La Folie in San Francisco, and Thomas Keller's Per Se before making Seattle his long game. Devoting a large chunk of his adult life to working for his mentors' mentors has helped

define his cooking at Copine and bring his international training to the neighborhood. The result? A polished restaurant with interesting and beautiful yet approachable food. Sign me up.

PICKLED CHANTERELLE MUSHROOMS

4 tsp extra-virgin olive oil (we prefer Moroccan)

6 oz chanterelle mushrooms, cleaned

1 cup water

¼ cup dry white wine

¼ cup champagne vinegar

1 dried chile de arbol

1 bay leaf

Pinch of ground cinnamon

VANILLA-SCENTED CORN SOUP

2 Tbsp unsalted butter

1 small yellow onion, thinly sliced

1 vanilla bean, split and scraped

5 ears corn, kernels removed from cobs

2 qts (8 cups) water

1½ cups heavy cream

Kosher salt

¼ cup popped popcorn, for garnish

Vanilla-Scented Corn Soup with Pickled Chanterelle Mushrooms

SERVES 4

While chanterelles are preferred, beech or any seasonal mushrooms make a good substitute.

PICKLED CHANTERELLE MUSHROOMS Heat oil in a skillet over medium heat, add mushrooms, and sauté for 5 minutes, until moisture has completely evaporated. Add water, wine, vinegar, chile, bay leaf, and cinnamon and bring to a simmer. Remove from heat and transfer mixture to a shallow pan to cool. Set aside to pickle for at least 1 hour. Discard bay leaf.

VANILLA-SCENTED CORN SOUP In a large saucepan, melt butter over low heat, add onion and vanilla, and sauté for 10 minutes, until the onion is translucent. Stir in corn and add enough water to cover the ingredients by 1 inch. Cook for 20 minutes, until corn is tender. (Add more water, if necessary.)

Working in batches, transfer mixture to a blender and blend until smooth. Using a fine-mesh strainer, strain liquid into a large bowl. (Be sure to get every bit of liquid from the pulp.)

Add cream and stir with a whisk until incorporated. Season with salt to taste.

PLATING Ladle soup into four bowls and arrange mushrooms on top. Garnish each bowl with 1 tablespoon of popcorn and serve hot or cold.

AIGRE-DOUX
¼ cup truffle juice
¼ cup granulated sugar
¼ cup glucose syrup
¼ cup sherry vinegar
1 Tbsp chopped black truffles, plus extra to garnish

QUAIL EGGS (OPTIONAL)
2 quail eggs
1 tsp crème fraîche
Fleur de sel
Shaved black truffles (we prefer Périgord), for garnish

RUSSET POTATO CHIPS
2 large russet potatoes, unpeeled and washed
Canola oil, for deep-frying
Salt

BEEF TARTARE
8 oz high-quality raw beef (we prefer Wagyu), finely chopped
1 Tbsp extra-virgin olive oil (Moroccan preferred), plus extra for dressing
2 tsp finely chopped shallot
2 tsp finely chopped red Fresno chiles
2 tsp finely chopped fresh chives
1½ tsp grated ginger
2 tsp sherry vinegar, or to taste
Fleur de sel, to taste
½ cup microgreens

Beef Tartare with Black Truffle Aigre-Doux and Russet Potato Chips

SERVES 4

High-quality beef is essential in this recipe. For the *aigre-doux*, McCrain recommends buying a can of preserved black winter truffle peelings in juice. The chips are best if handmade, but in a pinch, a good-quality plain potato chip makes a fair substitution.

AIGRE-DOUX In a small saucepan, combine all ingredients and heat over low heat for 20 minutes, until mixture reduces to a loose syrup. Remove from heat, allow to cool, and chill in the fridge.

QUAIL EGGS If making the quail eggs, bring a small saucepan of water to a boil, add quail eggs, and cook for 4 minutes. Chill in an ice bath, then peel and halve lengthwise. Remove yolks and put them into a small bowl. Add crème fraîche and a pinch of salt and mix well. Pipe the mixture into the egg whites and garnish with black truffle.

RUSSET POTATO CHIPS Slice potatoes using the thinnest setting on a mandoline, then put them into a colander. Rinse under cold water until water runs clear. Place chips on a clean dish towel and pat dry.

   Pour oil into a deep fryer or heavy stockpot (about 3 inches) and heat to a temperature of 275°F. Carefully lower potato slices and deep-fry in batches until crisp and golden brown. Using a slotted spoon, transfer chips to a plate lined with paper towels to cool and sprinkle with salt.

BEEF TARTARE Right before serving, combine beef, oil, shallot, chiles, chives, and ginger and mix well. Season to taste with vinegar and fleur de sel.

PLATING Put microgreens in a bowl and lightly dress with olive oil and a pinch of fleur de sel. Place tartare on four plates and garnish with chips, microgreens, quail egg, if using, and a drizzle of *aigre-doux*. Serve.

Dahlia Lounge Tom Douglas & Brock Johnson

TOM DOUGLAS was less than impressed with the "Godfather" title given to him in the nineties. As a fresh-faced 30-something who won his first of three James Beard Awards after opening his debut restaurant Dahlia Lounge, which has been helmed by chef Brock Johnson since 2009, he felt the moniker was misplaced. These days, he's cool with it. And with a dozen restaurants under his belt, he's engaged in the local food scene more than ever.

Douglas has remained a passionate chef ever since teaching himself how to cook by preparing meals from his favorite books. And while his culinary contributions include making crab cakes and triple coconut cream pie the unofficial foods of Seattle, his kitchen focus has evolved over the years. Providing for his crew and enticing the new brigade of cooks to come work for him has become a top priority (he was a major powerhouse behind the $15 minimum wage increase). He's an outspoken supporter of the food system: he grows vegetables on his 20-acre farm in

Prosser—photos of which adorn the walls of Dahlia and change seasonally—and he champions wild salmon.

For Johnson, sourcing from local farms is the basis of his cooking at Dahlia. "We try to take our farm's seasonal produce and really show it off," he says. "In spring, we serve buttered peas and baby greens with poached halibut and radishes. In the summer, it's tomato salad with stone fruits and herbs or Padrón peppers with freshly made soft cheeses. In the fall we coal-roast our delicata squashes and potatoes under applewood coals to accompany steaks and roasts."

Douglas, the Seattle icon who helped define Pacific Northwest cuisine, is now helping to define the next generation of chefs, like Johnson, simply leading by example. "We're so short on good cooks that they can demand higher wages and better benefits— things the restaurant industry was never known for," says Douglas. "I think it's awesome."

LEMON VINAIGRETTE

1 Tbsp freshly squeezed
   lemon juice

2 tsp finely chopped
   shallots

2 Tbsp extra-virgin olive oil

Kosher salt and freshly
   ground black pepper,
   to taste

DUNGENESS CRAB CAKES

1 lb fresh Dungeness
   crabmeat, drained and
   picked clean of shells

½ cup plus 2 Tbsp
   mayonnaise, preferably
   Hellmann's or Best Foods

2 Tbsp plus 2 tsp grated
   lemon zest

¼ cup finely chopped
   scallions, white and
   green parts

½ tsp kosher salt

¼ tsp freshly ground black
   pepper

2½ cups panko bread
   crumbs (divided)

5 Tbsp (½ stick plus 1 Tbsp)
   unsalted butter (divided)

ASSEMBLY

5 cups arugula leaves,
   washed and dried

4 lemon wedges

Dungeness Crab Cakes with Arugula and Lemon Vinaigrette

SERVES 4 (MAKES 8)

Chef Tom Douglas discovered the delight of sweet, briny, meaty Dungeness crab for the first time after moving to Seattle at the age of 19. He added fresh Dungeness crab cakes to his *Café Sport* menu, where they became an instant hit, and 35 years later, they are as popular as ever. Douglas uses panko (or Japanese) bread crumbs, which are coarser than ordinary bread crumbs but remain crisp once fried. Panko can be found in Japanese fish markets and many large supermarkets.

LEMON VINAIGRETTE In a small bowl, combine lemon juice and shallots and whisk in oil. Season to taste with salt and pepper.

DUNGENESS CRAB CAKES If crabmeat is wet, lightly squeeze the meat to remove excess moisture. In a large bowl, combine crabmeat, mayonnaise, lemon zest, scallions, salt, and pepper and mix with a rubber spatula. Add ½ cup panko and stir to combine.

Put remaining 2 cups panko in a shallow bowl. Form the crab mixture into eight patties, 1 inch thick, patting gently into shape. Put a patty into the panko and turn to coat both sides, patting it to shake off the excess. Transfer to a tray, then repeat with the remaining patties. Chill in the fridge for at least 1 hour.

Preheat oven to 450°F.

Set two large ovenproof skillets over medium-high heat and melt 2½ tablespoons butter in each pan. Add four crab cakes to each pan and fry for 1 minute. Place pans in the oven and cook for 6 minutes. Flip the crab cakes over, then cook for another 6 minutes, until heated through and golden brown on both sides.

ASSEMBLY Arrange two crab cakes on each plate. Put arugula in a bowl and toss with enough vinaigrette to coat leaves. (You may not need to use all the vinaigrette.) Season with salt to taste. Arrange a pile of arugula salad next to the crab cakes and add a lemon wedge. Serve immediately.

RIESLING DIP

½ cup dry Washington
   Riesling

¼ cup soy sauce

¼ cup rice vinegar

1 Tbsp granulated sugar

½ tsp grated ginger

¼ tsp finely chopped garlic

2 tsp finely chopped
   fresh chives

POT STICKERS

1 Tbsp sesame seeds

¾ lb peeled shrimp

1 Tbsp peanut oil

1½ cups thinly sliced
   shiitake mushroom caps

⅓ cup finely chopped
   carrots

2 Tbsp finely chopped
   scallions

2 Tbsp finely chopped
   fresh cilantro

2 tsp Chinese chili
   garlic paste

2 tsp grated ginger

1 tsp finely chopped garlic

1 tsp kosher salt

Cornstarch, for dusting

2 dozen wonton wrappers

Peanut or vegetable oil,
   for pan-frying

Shrimp and Shiitake Pot Stickers with Riesling Dip

SERVES 6 (MAKES 24)

The pot stickers can be assembled and poached early in the day. Simply keep them on a lightly oiled tray, covered with plastic wrap, in the fridge, until you are ready to pan-fry them.

RIESLING DIP In a small saucepan, combine Riesling, soy sauce, vinegar, sugar, ginger, and garlic and stir over medium heat, until sugar has dissolved. Remove from heat and set aside to cool. Add chives and chill in the fridge until needed.

POT STICKERS Toast sesame seeds in a small cast-iron skillet over medium heat, tossing continuously, until lightly browned and fragrant. Transfer to a small bowl and set aside.

If the shrimp meat is wet, lightly squeeze it to remove excess moisture. Place shrimp in a food processor and process until coarsely puréed. Heat peanut oil in a skillet over medium heat, add shiitakes and carrots, and sauté for 10 minutes, until softened. Remove from heat and set aside to cool.

In a large bowl, combine shrimp, shiitake mixture, scallions, cilantro, sesame seeds, chili garlic paste, ginger, garlic, and salt and mix well.

Line a baking sheet with parchment or wax paper and dust with cornstarch.

To form pot stickers, lay a wrapper on a clean work surface. Dip your index finger into a small bowl of water and wet the edges of the wrapper. Place a rounded tablespoon of filling in the center of the wrapper and bring two opposite points of the wrapper together to form a triangle. Press the edges together to seal. Lightly wet the two sealed edges and pinch to make a series of small pleats. (Make a pleat on one outer edge, followed by

a center pleat, and then a pleat on the other outer edge. Fill in gaps with a few pleats.) Place on the prepared baking sheet and continue until all the pot stickers are filled and sealed.

Fill a large pot with water and bring to a boil. Add pot stickers in batches (do not overcrowd them) and cook for 5 minutes, or until they float to the surface. Using a small sieve or slotted spoon, gently scoop the pot stickers out of the water and put them onto a baking sheet. Repeat with remaining pot stickers. (If they stick together, toss them with a little oil.)

Preheat oven to 200°F. Heat 2 tablespoons oil in a nonstick skillet over medium-high heat. Working in batches, add pot stickers to pan and pan-fry for 2 to 3 minutes, flip over, and cook for another 2 to 3 minutes, until lightly golden brown on both sides. Transfer to a baking sheet and keep warm in the oven until all pot stickers have been pan-fried.

Serve pot stickers immediately with ramekins of Riesling dip.

E. Smith Mercantile Jessie & Kate Poole

A THROWBACK to sweet turn-of-the-century Americana, this plucky and popular back bar—inside the fashionable E. Smith Mercantile—recently doubled its size to accommodate adoring fans who continuously sought respite at the original 14-seater. But what really makes this place tick are the Pooles themselves.

Neither Jessie nor her mom, Kate Poole, had any cocktail experience before opening the bar, but they were both adept social drinkers. (And it didn't hurt that they were both proficient in making their own tinctures and infusions.) What started with Jessie using her iPhone to Google recipes she wasn't familiar with is now a destination for cocktail lovers and connoisseurs.

The Pooles are masters at hospitality. They have created a brand that tells their story and reflects their strong sense of community and heritage—antique axes, a bunted, star-spangled flag from the eighteenth century, and taxidermy hang on the brick walls of

their historic Pioneer Square space. Everything at this bar is done with meticulous intention, and the first two drinks Jessie ever made at the bar remain on the menu today. There's Mary's Revenge, named after Jessie's great-grandmother who camped out at the local bar the morning after her husband, Elmer (E. Smith), told her he was going to "town" to get the mail and came home many hours later in a much altered state. It's made with champagne, quinine-flavored Byrrh, a sugar cube, and lavender bitters. There's also the Miner's Campfire, which uses smoke—E. Smith's signature flavor and scent profile—in the form of homemade bitters.

The food is a modern take on classic American comfort food, always aiming to draw inspiration from the natural bounty of the Pacific Northwest. "People ask us what kind of food we serve at E. Smith," says Jessie, "and our answer is always 'the good kind,' with a smile."

ROASTED PEPPERS
2 red bell peppers, seeded and stem and base trimmed

Olive oil, for drizzling

MAC AND CHEESE
¼ cup (½ stick) unsalted butter, plus extra for greasing

1 cup bread crumbs

¼ cup grated Pecorino Romano

1 clove garlic, finely chopped

¼ cup all-purpose flour

2 cups chicken stock

1 cup heavy cream

1 tsp salt, plus more for pasta water

1 tsp freshly ground black pepper

1 tsp smoked paprika

2 cups shredded cheddar

Roasted red bell peppers (see here)

16 oz fresh or dried pasta (about 4 cups)

Roasted Red Pepper Mac and Cheese

SERVES 6

Any fresh (or dried) pasta will work, but the Pooles like rigatoni for maximum cheesiness in every bite. This menu staple is a year-round favorite, even in the high heat of summer. Some comforts are worth sweating for.

ROASTED PEPPERS Set oven to broil. Line a baking sheet with parchment paper.

Lay peppers flat and skin side up on the prepared baking sheet. Drizzle lightly with oil and broil for 5 to 10 minutes, until skins are mostly black and blistered. Place peppers in a brown paper bag, close tightly, and set aside for 5 to 10 minutes. Gently peel off skins and discard. Slice peppers into ½-inch squares. Set aside.

MAC AND CHEESE Preheat oven to 350°F. Grease a 2-quart baking dish or six (10-ounce) ramekins and set aside.

In a small bowl, combine bread crumbs, Pecorino Romano, and garlic and set aside.

Melt the butter in a skillet over medium heat. Slowly whisk in flour and cook, stirring occasionally, for 3 to 4 minutes, until flour begins to brown. Pour in ½ cup chicken stock, whisking until smooth. Repeat until all stock is used.

Stir in cream, salt, pepper, and smoked paprika and bring to a boil. Reduce to medium-low heat and simmer, stirring occasionally, until thickened enough to coat the back of a wooden spoon. Fold in cheddar until melted and remove from heat.

Bring a large pot of water to a boil, add 1½ tablespoons salt, and cook pasta for 2 to 3 minutes (6 to 8 minutes if using dry pasta) until very al dente (to prevent it from going mushy when reheated). Drain, transfer to a large bowl, and stir in cheese sauce and roasted peppers. Toss until well coated.

Transfer pasta to baking dish(es) and top with bread crumb mixture. Cover with foil, place on a baking sheet, and cook for 15 to 20 minutes. Remove foil and bake for another 10 minutes, until bread crumbs are lightly browned and sauce is bubbly. Rest for 5 to 10 minutes, then serve.

SMOKY COCCHI

1 (750-ml) bottle Cocchi
Americano
¼ cup Lapsang Souchong
tea leaves

SMOKED OLIVES IN BRINE

2 cups hickory or
applewood chips, soaked
in water for 30 minutes
1 (10-oz) jar Castelvetrano
olives in brine

SMOKY MARTINI

2 oz gin
¾ oz Smoky Cocchi
(see here)
¼ oz smoked olive brine
(see here, or we suggest
using Stopsky's)
Drop of E. Smith Mercantile
Smoke Bitters
2 smoked Castelvetrano
olives, for garnish
(see here)

Smoky Martini

SERVES 1

"Smoke has been a
signature flavor, scent,
and source of inspira-
tion at E. Smith Mercan-
tile," says Jessie Poole.
"Whether a backyard
campfire or from a
smoke stack billowing
from a log cabin, it
evokes nostalgia of a
simpler time."

SMOKY COCCHI Pour Cocchi and tea into a nonreactive container and steep at room temperature overnight. (Reserve bottle for later use.) Take a sip in the morning to test its smokiness and steep longer if necessary.

Strain tea through a fine-mesh strainer and pour the smoky Cocchi back into its original bottle. Store in the fridge for up to six months.

SMOKED OLIVES IN BRINE Pat wood chips dry and add a handful to a smoker box. (Alternatively, put chips into a heatproof pan and cover with a piece of foil. Pierce holes throughout, 2 inches apart, to allow the smoke to waft out.) Turn gas grill on to a low setting, place smoker box (or pan) on rack, and close the lid. (If you're using a charcoal grill, throw the soaked chips directly onto the hot coals.)

Put olives and brine into a cast-iron skillet, reserving the jar. Once smoke emerges from the grill, place pan next to the smoke box and close the grill's lid. Smoke for 30 to 60 minutes, adding additional chips if needed.

Put olives and brine back into the jar. Store in the fridge for up to six months (the longer you keep them in the jar, the smokier they will be).

SMOKY MARTINI Put a martini glass in the fridge or freezer for 1 hour.

Pour gin and Cocchi into a mixing glass and top with enough ice to cover (three-quarters full). Using a bar spoon, stir until cold, keeping the curve of the spoon against the inside of the glass to create a spinning motion with the ice. (Be sure to grip the glass from the base so that the heat of your hand doesn't work against you.)

Add olive brine and bitters to your chilled martini glass and gently rotate, tipping the glass at approximately 45 degrees to coat the inside. Strain cock-tail into glass and garnish with olives.

Gracia Chester Gerl

BACK WHEN he was the chef at Place Pigalle, Chester Gerl would occasionally toss some Mexican flair into the restaurant's daily specials, in the ilk of guajillo sauce with a piece of halibut. Owner Bill Frank often reminded him, "This is not a Mexican restaurant!"

Years later, Gerl moved across the street to Matt's in the Market and had a chance encounter with James Beard Award–winning chef Jonathan Waxman that would change the trajectory of his career from seafood to Mexican food. Waxman not only helped Gerl land a job with restaurateur Marc Meyer in New York (Hundred Acres and Rosie's), he also encouraged Gerl to open his own Mexican restaurant after experiencing his cuisine firsthand. That was in 2013. In 2016, Gerl returned to Seattle and opened Gracia on Ballard Avenue.

The Huarache (masa cake, duck carnitas, charred salsa roja) and Octopus al Pastor topped with grilled pineapple and roasted chiles have emerged as crowd favorites, but it's the homemade tortillas, made with heirloom corn sourced from small Oaxacan farms, that are the axis of Gracia. In fact, one of the most enviable seats in the restaurant is at the open-kitchen counter where you witness the masa-making in action. And with an aesthetic inspired by his many trips to Mexico, Gracia serves up authentic central and southern Mexico–focused cuisine that allows Gerl the freedom to finally put the food he loves onto a menu.

SALSA MACHA

2 cups canola oil

5 Tbsp sesame seeds

1 Tbsp pepitas

2 Tbsp sunflower seeds

2 Tbsp peanuts

2 Tbsp almonds

3 guajillo chiles, stemmed and seeded

3 Puya chiles, stemmed and seeded

3 ancho chiles, stemmed and seeded

3 chipotles, stemmed and seeded

4 cloves garlic, sliced

¼ cup apple cider vinegar

2 Tbsp sea salt

CHIPS

3 qts (12 cups) canola oil

½ (25-oz) package high-quality corn tortillas, quartered

Salt, to taste

Salsa Macha with Chips

SERVES 8 TO 10

This very versatile sauce is used as an actual salsa at the restaurant, but it also makes a great marinade or glaze for meats and fish. Just be sure to remove the stems and seeds from all the chiles.

SALSA MACHA Combine oil, seeds, and nuts in a saucepan set over medium heat, bring to a simmer, and cook for 3 minutes, or until the nuts are golden brown. Add the chiles and cook for another minute. Add garlic and simmer for another minute until browned. Carefully stir in vinegar (it could splatter) and salt, then set aside to cool. Transfer mixture to a blender and purée until smooth. Leftovers can be stored in the fridge for up to two weeks.

CHIPS Pour oil into a large saucepan or a deep fryer and heat to a temperature of 300°F. Carefully lower tortillas into oil and stir continuously until bubbles subside. Using a slotted spoon, transfer chips to a plate lined with paper towels. Season with salt and set aside to cool.

Serve tortilla chips with salsa macha.

OCTOPUS
2 gallons water
1 cup salt
5 fresh bay leaves
3 to 4 lbs fresh sustainable octopus, such as Spanish (see Note)

ROAST POTATOES
1 lb Yukon Gold potatoes, peeled
2 Tbsp olive oil
Sea salt, to taste

SALSA VERDE
2 large poblano chiles
½ bunch fresh Italian parsley, plus extra for garnish
1 clove garlic
Zest of 2 limes
1 canned anchovy fillet
1½ tsp sea salt
1 Tbsp apple cider vinegar
¼ cup canola oil
2 Tbsp olive oil

Note: Fresh Spanish octopus can be found at Uwajimaya, Pure Food Fish Market, Pike Place Fish Market, and City Fish Co.

Braised Octopus with Poblano Chile Salsa Verde

SERVES 4

OCTOPUS Bring water and salt to a boil in a large saucepan and add bay leaves. Carefully lower octopus into water (to allow the tentacles to curl) and submerge entirely. Reduce heat and simmer for 1 hour, until tender.

ROAST POTATOES Preheat oven to 350°F.

Put potatoes into a stockpot, add enough cold water to cover, and salt generously. Bring to a boil over high heat, then reduce heat to medium-low, and simmer for 25 to 30 minutes, until fork tender. Drain, then set aside to cool. Quarter potatoes and place on a baking sheet. Add oil, toss to coat, and season with salt. Bake for 20 to 25 minutes until golden brown (no need to toss). Set aside.

SALSA VERDE Preheat oven to 400°F.

Put chiles onto a baking sheet and roast for 8 to 10 minutes, until skins blister. Set aside to cool, then carefully wipe off the outer skin and remove seeds.

In a food processor, combine chiles, parsley, garlic, lime zest, anchovy, sea salt, and vinegar. With the food processor running, gradually add oils and blend until emulsified. Set aside.

ASSEMBLY Drain octopus and set aside to cool. Remove beak and head and discard. Slice tentacles into ¼-inch chunks and set aside.

In a large bowl, combine warm potatoes, octopus, and 3 to 4 spoonfuls of salsa verde and toss. Garnish with parsley and serve with more salsa verde on the side.

Heartwood Provisions Varin Keokitvon & Amanda Reed

IN 2016, when Seattle's craft cocktail movement was a little, well, stagnant, Heartwood Provisions was considered ambitious. "Heartwood started out as a tavern concept, but it transformed along the way," says chef Varin Keokitvon. "We took the best of what Amanda does and what I do and tried to bridge that gap." His partner in crime—beverage director Amanda Reed—left her job as general/bar manager of Tavern Law to help launch the new project.

They began pairing dishes with innovative cocktails as a sort of drinkable garnish meant to enhance flavors that might otherwise be obscured. "Varin's beautiful food was a selling point," explains Reed, "and it was an enticing opportunity." An admitted Busch drinker on the regular, Keokitvon found it inspiring to learn that cocktails could have a positive influence on his food. "In the past, pairings lacked sophistication—a duck dish with cherries might have been served with a Manhattan because it had a cherry in it. Amanda takes it to another level to harmonize the experience—it doesn't take over the quality of the dish, and that's pretty cool."

Keokitvon was previously the head chef of retail operations at FareStart and trained at El Celler de Can Roca in Spain. With a lively and warm ambience denoted by a large open kitchen, massive rounded bar, and wine-stocked walls, Heartwood has become a popular downtown destination for business meetings, happy hours, and date nights. "Even though it's not for everybody, the cocktail pairings create a conversation," says Reed. "It allows people to engage in, and be in the moment with, the dining experience."

→ Heartwood Yellowtail

SIMPLE SYRUP

1 cup granulated sugar

1 cup water

AVOCADO PURÉE

2 very ripe avocados

3 Tbsp simple syrup
(see here)

Juice of 1 lemon

1 tsp salt

**PRESERVED LEMON–
PIMENTON VINAIGRETTE**

¼ cup olive oil

¼ cup canola oil

Juice of 1½ lemons

2 Tbsp preserved lemons,
seeds removed and
chopped (see Note)

2 Tbsp finely chopped
shallots

1 Tbsp Dijon mustard

2 tsp granulated sugar

2 tsp smoked paprika
(pimenton de la Vera)
(see Note)

1 tsp salt

YELLOWTAIL

1 (1-lb) sushi-grade
yellowtail (hamachi) fillet,
blood line removed (ask
your fishmonger)

1 to 2 tsp Maldon sea salt

1 cup avocado purée
(see here)

1 ruby red grapefruit,
segmented and cut into
½-inch pieces

½ cup Castelvetrano olives,
pitted and halved

¼ cup micro purple radish

1 (1-inch) piece horseradish

¼ cup high-quality olive oil
(we prefer Arbequina)

1 cup preserved lemon–
pimenton vinaigrette
(see here)

*Note: Preserved lemons can
be found at specialty grocers
or online. Pimenton de la Vera
is a Spanish smoked paprika
that can be found in the spice
section of your local market. It
should not be confused with
other types of paprika.*

Heartwood Yellowtail

SERVES 4 TO 6

The freshest available fish will enhance the quality of this dish. Look for yellowtail (also known as hamachi) at a quality fishmonger or a Japanese market specializing in sashimi-grade fish. Inspired by Mediterranean flavors, this dish should be finished with a high-quality olive oil that will enhance the flavors dramatically.

SIMPLE SYRUP Mix sugar and water in a small saucepan over medium heat. Bring to a simmer, stirring, until sugar is fully dissolved. (The simple syrup can be stored in the fridge for up to two weeks.)

AVOCADO PURÉE Put all ingredients into a high-power blender and blend on high speed until smooth. (Alternatively, use an immersion blender.)

Place in a piping bag or a container covered with plastic wrap. (Be sure the plastic contacts the purée to prevent it from oxidizing or turning brown and dull.) Set aside.

PRESERVED LEMON–PIMENTON VINAIGRETTE Combine oils in a bowl and mix. Set aside.

In a high-power blender (such as a Vitamix), combine all ingredients except oils and blend for 1 minute. With the blender running, gradually add oil and blend until emulsified. (Alternatively, use an immersion blender.) Set aside.

YELLOWTAIL To prepare yellowtail, cut into 1½-inch squares that are ¼ inch thick. Pat fish dry with paper towel, then place on serving plates and season with salt.

Pipe dots of avocado purée and vinaigrette randomly all over the yellowtail. (Alternatively, smear purée on plates or spoon it on top of the fish.)

Scatter grapefruit and olives over fish and top with micro radish.

Using a microplane, grate horseradish over the servings. Drizzle with olive oil and serve chilled.

¾ oz Hayman's Old Tom gin

½ oz freshly squeezed
   lemon juice

¼ oz simple syrup
   (see page 58)

Dash of Scrappy's
   celery bitters

1 oz sparkling wine
   (we prefer Cava)

Heartwood Yellowtail
Cocktail Pairing

SERVES 1

This refreshing cocktail complements the bright and fresh flavors of the yellowtail, while fresh lemon and sparkling wine subdue the spicy elements and bring the flavors together. The lasting finish completes the dish.

Combine all ingredients, excluding sparkling wine, in a mixing glass or tin. Add ice and shake for 20 seconds. Fine-strain ingredients into a cocktail glass. Top with sparkling wine.

Hello Robin Robin Wehl Martin

THE ONLY thing Robin Wehl Martin loves more than baking cookies is sharing them with the Capitol Hill neighborhood she's called home for 20 years. Before opening her shop, the mother of three (who describes herself as having an excessive baking problem) would feverishly bake cookies and other treats and drop them off on neighbors' doorsteps. In 2013, Wehl Martin, along with her husband, Clay Martin, opened Hello Robin on the corner of 19th and Mercer.

With its shop name inspired by the famous *Seinfeld* line "Hello, Newman," Hello Robin features freshly baked cookies and a walk-up scoop shop with ice cream sandwiches galore. All-time favorites include salty butterscotch, flourless Mexican chocolate, and birthday cake. There's also the wildly popular Mackles'more: cookie dough baked on a graham cracker and topped with chocolate, which fellow neighbor Macklemore has tried on numerous occasions. (On one occasion, Wehl Martin even dropped

one into his trick-or-treat bag, but that's another story.) Chocolate chip, however, is the signature cookie here. "If I have people over for dinner and the food isn't as good as I'd like it to be," says Wehl Martin, "I'll immediately make a batch of chocolate chip cookies to erase that memory!"

There are no rules at Hello Robin, which is a large part of its success. Wehl Martin uses whatever wild flavor concoctions she's inspired by at the time, whether it be wasabi or some other ingredient that has caught her eye at the market. She is also often in the shop, making the cookies in her open kitchen, where she can put on a show and talk to neighbors at the same time. This is cookie therapy at its finest.

¾ cup (1½ sticks)
   unsalted butter

½ cup packed brown sugar

½ cup granulated sugar

1½ tsp vanilla extract

1 egg

1½ cups all-purpose flour

1 cup instant oats

¾ tsp baking soda

½ tsp ground cinnamon

½ tsp kosher salt

1 cup chocolate chips

1 cup dried tart cherries,
   raisins or walnuts
   (optional)

Oatmeal Cookies

MAKES 24 COOKIES

This recipe is packed with chocolate chunks and dried tart cherries, making arguably the perfect oatmeal cookies.

Preheat oven to 375°F. Line a baking sheet with parchment paper.

In a stand mixer fitted with a paddle attachment, cream butter and sugars. Add vanilla and egg.

In a separate bowl, combine flour, oats, baking soda, cinnamon, and salt and mix well. Slowly add flour mixture to butter mixture and mix well. Stir in chocolate chips and dried fruit or nuts, if using.

Scoop cookie dough (about 1 tablespoon per spoonful) onto the prepared baking sheet, then bake for 9 to 12 minutes until light brown around the edges. (Do not overbake!) Let cool on pan before eating.

½ cup good-quality
   semisweet chocolate
   chips
1 cup (2 sticks) plus
   2 Tbsp unsalted butter
3 eggs
4 tsp vanilla extract
1½ cups all-purpose flour
2¼ cups granulated sugar
½ cup cocoa powder

¾ tsp kosher salt
2 tubs of your favorite
   premium ice cream
   (we prefer Molly Moon's,
   of course)

Brownie (Ice Cream) Sandwiches

SERVES 12

Robin Wehl Martin's brownies are super-moist and extra thin because they're poured onto a sheet pan and later filled (sandwiched) with ice cream. As she explains, "It is firm enough to hold ice cream, but soft enough to bite into without breaking your teeth!"

Preheat oven to 375°F. Line a rimmed 18- × 13-inch baking sheet with enough parchment paper to extend over the sides (for easy removal).

Put chocolate chips and butter into a microwave-safe measuring cup or bowl and microwave for 1 minute, until melted. Stir until smooth, then set aside to cool. Add eggs, one at a time, and vanilla, stirring to combine.

In a large bowl, combine flour, sugar, cocoa powder, and salt. Pour chocolate mixture into flour mixture and stir until smooth.

Pour batter into the prepared baking sheet and bake for 15 to 20 minutes, or until the top feels firm. (Do not overbake, otherwise the brownies will end up dry!) Set aside to cool, then refrigerate until chilled. (Alternatively, cut immediately into squares and top with a heaping scoop of ice cream.)

Turn the brownie slab onto a cutting board, cut into 24 equal squares, and freeze until ready to serve.

ASSEMBLY Top 12 squares with ice cream and press another square on top of each to form sandwiches. Serve immediately.

Hitchcock Brendan McGill

WHILE NOT *technically* located in Seattle (but only a 30-minute ferry ride away), Hitchcock on Bainbridge Island is where diners go when they want a transcendent dining experience. Sure, this charming neighborhood restaurant would do well in the city, but that would take away from its essence.

Being on the island provides chef-owner Brendan McGill an abundance of fresh, local goodies at his fingertips. "Mama B" harvests wild watercress and red currant bushes on her own property especially for Hitchcock, and another neighbor brings in fresh figs from her trees. A picturesque walnut orchard near McGill's own home assures him a lifetime supply of homemade *nocino* (walnut liqueur), while gorgeous farms dedicated to organic, holistic farming—including an oyster micro-farm on the sound—are just a few miles away from the restaurant.

Hitchcock has sprouted not only two namesake delis—one next door to the restaurant and the other in Georgetown—but also a more casual café (Cafe Hitchcock) and a pizzeria (Bruciato). All five businesses showcase some of the best charcuterie in town, a few of them made from the Mangalitsa pigs raised by McGill. (Notably, fennel *lonza*—a type of cured pork loin with pickled fennel, toasted pine nuts, and olive oil—is available at Hitchcock.) High-quality ingredients such as these speak to the integrity McGill brings to everything he does. And it's what makes this culinary experience worth seeking out.

→ Roast Chicken with Bitter Green Salad

ROAST CHICKEN

1 (3- to 4-lb) high-quality
  organic, pasture-raised
  whole chicken
1½ cups kosher salt, plus
  extra for finishing
1 cup granulated sugar
1 bunch fresh thyme
1 bay leaf
1 tsp fennel seeds

1 tsp whole black
  peppercorns
1 tsp coriander seeds
2 Tbsp cultured butter,
  room temperature
1 tsp wildflower honey

Roast Chicken with Bitter Green Salad

SERVES 2 TO 4

Before the chef's tasting menu took center stage, Hitchcock was more of a neighborhood restaurant with the brined roast half chicken as the main draw. The wood-fired oven helps, but it's an excellent-quality chicken that is essential to this dish.

ROAST CHICKEN Using sharp scissors, cut out the backbone from the chicken. Using a sharp knife, make an incision down the center of the breast, on both sides of the keel bone. Using the heel of the knife, crack through the wishbone, separating the halves of the chicken from the keel. Using your fingers, carefully pull the remaining wishbone from the chicken breast. Fold the wing tip back behind its shoulders. (The chicken should be halved in two, with each breast still connected to the hindquarter by its skin.) Chill in the fridge.

Combine salt, sugar, herbs, and spices in a saucepan. Add 4 cups water and bring to a boil. Reduce heat to medium-low and simmer 1 hour. Strain the brine into a large bowl, and add enough ice and water until you have 2 quarts of cool brine.

Submerge the chicken into the brine and refrigerate for 3 hours, placing small plates on top of the chicken to keep it submerged. Remove chicken from brine and transfer to a plate. Refrigerate overnight, uncovered. (Brining ensures a moist and juicy chicken, and the refrigeration helps to create a tacky pellicle on the skin that crisps up brilliantly.)

Preheat a convection oven (or wood-fired oven) to 500°F.

Combine butter and honey in a small bowl and beat together using a teaspoon. Using your fingers, thoroughly rub this mixture into the chicken skin, distributing it evenly. Place chicken in a pan with a roasting rack and roast for 15 to 20 minutes, or until cooked at the joint and aggressively blistered. Set aside to rest for 5 minutes.

EMULSIFIED APPLE CIDER VINAIGRETTE

1 cup apple cider vinegar

1 Tbsp Dijon mustard

1½ tsp salt

1 egg

2 cups canola oil

½ cup extra-virgin olive oil

SALAD

4 cups peppery or bitter greens

Shaved raw vegetables, such as radish, turnip, asparagus, and/or Romanesco broccoli

Emulsified apple cider vinaigrette (see here), to taste

EMULSIFIED APPLE CIDER VINAIGRETTE In a high-power blender (such as a Vitamix), combine all ingredients except oil and blend until smooth. With the blender running, gradually add oil and blend until emulsified. The vinaigrette can be stored in the fridge for up to three months.

SALAD Combine greens and shaved vegetables in a large bowl, add vinaigrette to taste, and toss lightly.

ASSEMBLY Remove the chicken's hindquarters and separate drumsticks from thighs. Carve the rib off each breast but leave wing attached (this is called a chicken supreme). Serve with salad.

1 lb high-quality skin-on wild king or sockeye salmon, thawed if frozen and pinbones removed (see Note)

¾ cup kosher salt

½ cup granulated sugar

1 tsp coriander seeds, toasted and ground

1 tsp fennel seeds

Zest of ½ lemon

2 to 3 sprigs fresh thyme, leaves only

2 to 3 sprigs fresh Italian parsley, leaves only

2 to 3 sprigs fresh dill, coarsely chopped

Wood chips (we prefer applewood)

Cold-Smoked King Salmon

SERVES 4 TO 8

Chef Brendan McGill uses local king salmon and applewood to smoke it. Rather than being smoked in the tradition of Native Americans, the salmon is cured with salt and sugar, then seasoned with a hint of wood smoke, and served with one of the assembly options here. "This is a Northwest classic through the lens of Scandinavian gravlax," says McGill. "I recommend using a smoking gun when preparing this at home."

Pat salmon dry with a paper towel. Line a shallow dish with a sheet of plastic wrap double its length.

Combine salt, sugar, spices, lemon zest, and herbs in a food processor and blend until smooth. Pour half of the cure into the prepared dish, place salmon—skin side down—on top, then pour the remaining cure over it. Rub cure all over fish. Fold both sides of the plastic wrap over the salmon and refrigerate for three to five days, depending on how well you like your fish cured (McGill prefers three days). Flip the fish each day. Check readiness after three days by giving the fish a little squeeze. If the thinnest part of the fillet (e.g., the tail) starts to feel firm like jerky, remove fish from cure. If it feels soft in the center on day three, cure the salmon for the entire five days.

Rinse fillet under cold running water, then pat dry with paper towels and place on a roasting rack set on top of a baking sheet. Put on the top shelf of your fridge and refrigerate for 24 hours, uncovered (to form a pellicle for the smoke to adhere to).

To prepare the fish for smoking, place a small roasting or steamer rack in a deep casserole or other deep dish (to create a smoke chamber) and place fish on top. Run a smoker tube along the inside of the bowl, then seal the bowl with plastic wrap.

ASSEMBLY 1 (OPTIONAL)
Bagels or rye bread
Capers
Red onion
Sieved hard-boiled eggs

ASSEMBLY 2 (OPTIONAL)
Cultured butter or whipped
  crème fraîche
Assorted pickles
Fresh berries
Preserved mushrooms,
  pasteurized in oil

ASSEMBLY 3 (OPTIONAL)
Pickled onions
Arugula or pea tendrils
Capers

Note: The health department suggests freezing salmon before serving it undercooked. Without the "kill" step of heat, any potentially harmful microorganisms in the flesh will be killed after being frozen for 24 hours. And because salmon is high in fat, the freezing will have minimal effect on the texture. (You can purchase previously frozen salmon as a safety measure.) Smoke is also an excellent antibacterial.

Set that bowl into a larger bowl filled with ice and you'll have a nice cool chamber into which you can periodically add smoke to keep it nice and smoky. (Alternatively, buy a cold-smoke generator and install it in an outdoor barrel smoker, or in the side of an old non-working fridge by the woodshed.)

Smoke for 4 hours, keeping the temperature of the smoke set-up under 100°F. Remove the smoked fish from your smoker and refrigerate overnight, uncovered.

ASSEMBLY Serve in a classic New York style with bagel (or rye bread), capers, red onion, and sieved eggs. Alternatively, serve it with cultured butter or whipped crème fraîche, assorted pickles, fresh berries, and/or preserved mushrooms. It also makes an excellent tartine with pickled onions, arugula (or pea tendrils), and capers.

Jack's BBQ Jack Timmons

WITH THREE 22-foot-long smokers pluming out back, you can smell Jack's before you even pull up into the driveway. Inside diners are transported to an Austin roadhouse-inspired dining room dotted with string lights—a Texas patio staple—and a roomy bar that starts serving at 11 am. This is the place where you kick off your boots, throw back a martini with pickled okra, and stay awhile.

Jack Timmons, a Texas native and barbecue junkie, shed his tech consultant persona when he first launched a series of pop-ups called Seattle Brisket Experience (he's a big Jimi Hendrix fan) and valiantly recreated Central Texas barbecue in the Northwest. He was so committed to nailing the barbecue game that he had the pitmaster from famed barbecue joint Louie Mueller come help him open Jack's in 2014.

To this day, his pit crew is based on the Mueller method: they don't use thermometers to test the doneness of meat; instead, it's all done by touch. The meat is also only seasoned with salt and pepper, which delights diners who are rediscovering barbecue or, at the very least, a different style. "Many Seattleites think barbecue is all about the sauce," says Timmons. "They're often surprised when they come here and see the sauce on the side, or none at all."

If they do indulge in sauce, it is sopped up with slices of white bread, and served alongside classic fixings such as collard greens and mac and cheese. The beef ribs fly off Jack's menu, but the joint is renowned for their two-day-smoked brisket. Barbecue is not something Seattle is known for, but Timmons is certainly changing that.

CHILI

4 ancho chiles, stemmed

1 chipotle, stemmed

1 chile de arbol, stemmed

1 onion, chopped

3 cloves garlic

6 Tbsp paprika

2 tsp cumin seeds, toasted and ground

2 tsp chili powder

Pinch of red pepper flakes

2 Tbsp salt, plus extra to taste

1 Tbsp freshly ground black pepper, plus extra to taste

3 lbs beef, such as smoked brisket, chuck, or tri-tip, cut into ½-inch pieces

1 Tbsp canola oil

GARNISH

Shredded cheddar

1 small white onion, chopped

Pickled jalapeño peppers

Sour cream

Jack's Texas Red Chili

SERVES 6 TO 8

When Jack Timmons opened the restaurant, he rediscovered an old cookbook that his parents gave him when he went to college. "The first page had a chili recipe from Frank X. Tolbert, the cofounder of the Original Terlingua International Championship Chili Cookoff," says Timmons. "Inspired by his use of whole chili pods, we created this recipe."

CHILI Put chiles, onion, and garlic into a large Dutch oven, add just enough water to cover, and bring to a boil over high heat. Cover and let steep for 10 minutes, or until softened. Add paprika, cumin, chili powder, red pepper flakes, salt and pepper.

Lightly season beef with salt and pepper. Heat oil in a large skillet over medium-high heat and add beef. Sear for 5 minutes, until browned. Add beef to chile mixture and enough water to cover. Simmer for 45 minutes, occasionally using a heatproof potato masher to mix meat and spices. Set aside to cool and refrigerate overnight to intensify flavor.

Reheat chili in a large pot over medium heat. Ladle hot chili into bowls, top with cheddar, onion, and pickled jalapeño peppers. Serve with sour cream on the side.

DRESSING

1 Tbsp granulated sugar

1 cup white vinegar

1 cup canola oil

1 Tbsp fresh oregano

1 Tbsp Worcestershire sauce

1 tsp freshly ground black pepper

Salt, to taste

SALAD

3 (16-oz) cans black-eyed peas, rinsed

2 (16-oz) cans corn, rinsed

1 (4-oz) jar pimentos, chopped (including liquid)

1 bunch scallions, diced

1 green bell pepper, finely chopped

1 red bell pepper, finely chopped

1 yellow bell pepper, finely chopped

1 onion, chopped

½ bunch fresh Italian parsley, chopped

3 cloves garlic, finely chopped

2 Tbsp finely chopped jalapeño peppers

Salt and pepper, to taste

1 avocado, pitted and chopped, for garnish

Tortilla chips, to serve

Texas Caviar

SERVES 6 TO 8

"This is an old family recipe that's best when prepared a day in advance," Timmons says. "My sister garnishes it with chopped avocado, and we scoop it up with Fritos or tortilla chips."

DRESSING Combine ingredients in a bowl and mix well.

SALAD Combine all ingredients except avocado and tortilla chips in a large bowl, and toss to mix. Add vinaigrette, adjust seasoning to taste, and garnish with avocado. Serve with tortilla chips.

Kedai Makan Kevin Burzell

IN MALAYSIA, *kedai makan* essentially means "eat shop," but it's so much more than that. For one, these types of small Malaysian restaurants are where Kevin Burzell and his partner Alysson Wilson spent a lot of time researching and amassing loads of inspiration for the restaurant that would someday be theirs. The two were living in Germany at the time and met Rachel Marshall, who had just started selling her ginger beer at farmers' markets in Seattle. She not only convinced them to sell their Malaysian food at the markets, she tipped them off to the walk-up window next to her Capitol Hill bar, Montana.

After years of working in the kitchens of Poppy (page 126), Monsoon, and Ba Bar, Burzell finally had a brick-and-mortar space, albeit the tiniest one in the city. He cooked in comically cramped conditions for more than two years until they moved into the La Bête space around the corner. The couple kept the hand-crafted tables and strung up some Chinese lanterns

around the bar. Photos of their travels adorn the deep turquoise walls—the same color scheme as the walk-up. And while the modest decorations evoke nostalgia, the boldly flavored dishes speak to present time and place.

Burzell is in the kitchen every night. As his menu evolves, there are several signatures dishes that will always remain: specifically the *nasi goreng* (fried rice with tofu, bean sprouts, and cucumbers topped with a fried egg and sweet soy sauce) and *chili pan mee* (wheat noodles, ground pork, poached egg, and fried anchovies). The restaurant honors Malaysia as its muse by being a buzzy, redolent hub with a refreshing mix of authentic flavors and varied cultures. You can stuff yourself and have a beer for less than $20 and walk out totally satisfied. A rare find in Seattle.

→ Kerabu Taugeh and Mackerel Stuffed
   with Rempah and Air Assam

DRESSING

2 bird's eye chiles

2 cloves garlic

½ shallot, finely chopped

2 oz fresh tamarind pulp, soaked in ¾ cup water until soft

½ cup fish sauce

2 Tbsp granulated sugar

Freshly squeezed lime juice (optional)

SALAD

10 oz mung bean sprouts, washed and stems removed

¼ cup fresh mint, torn

¼ cup fresh Thai basil leaves, torn

¼ cup laksa leaf (*rau ram*), torn

¼ cup *kersik* (toasted grated coconut)

Lime wedges, to serve

Kerabu Taugeh
(Sprout Salad with Tamarind Dressing)

SERVES 2 TO 4

Hard-to-find southeast Asian ingredients can often be found at Viet-Wah on Jackson and Lam's Seafood Market on King Street. You can use cilantro instead of laksa leaf—or any combination of herbs—depending on what's readily available.

DRESSING Using a mortar and pestle, pound chiles, garlic, and shallot together. Set aside.

In a bowl, mix tamarind and water until it forms a thick paste. Strain tamarind paste to remove the seeds and any fibers. Add chile mixture, fish sauce, and sugar and mix well. Adjust seasoning to taste. (The dressing should be sour, salty, and slightly pungent. If you want it sweeter, add more sugar. If you want more sourness, add more tamarind or a bit of lime juice.) The dressing can be stored in the fridge for up to a week.

SALAD Combine ingredients in a bowl and mix well. Add half of the dressing, toss, and taste. Adjust seasoning, if needed. Garnish with lime wedges and serve immediately.

REMPAH (SPICE PASTE)

7 dried bird's eye chiles

1 dried California chile

¾ oz galangal, peeled and finely chopped

1½ tsp kosher salt

1 lemongrass stalk, trimmed of tough outer and top leaves, finely chopped

1 oz fresh turmeric, peeled and finely chopped

4 cloves garlic, finely chopped

1 shallot, finely chopped

2 Tbsp vegetable or peanut oil

AIR ASSAM (SOUR WATER)

3 bird's eye chiles

1 shallot, thinly sliced

½ tsp *belacan* or shrimp paste (we prefer Blachen Dried Shrimp Paste)

¼ cup tamarind pulp, soaked in 1 cup of water until softened

½ Tbsp granulated sugar

1 Tbsp *kecap manis* (see Note)

1 Tbsp freshly squeezed lime juice

MACKEREL

1 whole mackerel, cleaned

Salt

Ground turmeric (optional)

Banana leaf, washed (optional)

Lime wedges, to serve

Steamed rice, to serve

Note: Kecap manis is a thick, sweet soy sauce made with palm sugar and can be found at most Asian food stores.

Mackerel Stuffed with Rempah and Air Assam

SERVES 2 TO 4

Air assam is a tangy, savory, and slightly sweet dipping sauce. Despite the use of chiles, it's not very spicy. It's the perfect complement to an oily fish like mackerel.

REMPAH Soak dried chiles in warm water for 30 minutes. Remove stem and seeds from chiles, then finely chop. (Leave the seeds in if you want the rempah spicier.)

Using a mortar and pestle, pound galangal and the salt together. Add lemongrass and pound to a fine consistency. Add the chiles, then turmeric, garlic, and shallot. (Be sure to pound it well each time.)

Heat oil in a small skillet over medium heat, add paste, and fry for 6 to 8 minutes, until fragrant and the color turns ruby red. Set aside to cool.

AIR ASSAM Using a mortar and pestle, pound chiles, shallot, and *belacan* together, just until shallots are broken up but chunky.

Using your hands, break up tamarind and mix with the water until it forms a thick paste. Strain the paste into the pounded ingredients. Add sugar, *kecap manis*, and lime juice. Taste and adjust seasoning, if needed. (It should be sour, spicy, and mildly sweet.)

MACKEREL Preheat oven to 450°F.

Cut mackerel along the length of the backbone, ½ inch deep, creating a pocket to stuff the rempah in. Season with salt and turmeric, if using.

Stuff rempah in mackerel, place on a baking sheet, and cook for 10 to 13 minutes, until cooked through. (Alternatively, steam in a banana leaf–lined steamer for 15 minutes or wrap fish in a banana leaf and grill over hot coals for 18 minutes.)

PLATING Serve mackerel with air assam, lime wedges, and steamed rice.

Little Fish Zoi Antonitsas

ZOI ANTONITSAS has always been a hustler. She made a name for herself on *Top Chef* season four and more recently as one of *Food & Wine*'s Best New Chefs, but her fierceness emerged back when she was 16, when she parlayed her job as a barista into her first restaurant gig as a summer prep cook at Dahlia Lounge (page 42). She soon followed that up with a stint at Etta's and then in 2010, she became chef at Madison Park Conservatory, owned by Cormac Mahoney and Bryan Jarr.

Though the restaurant closed three years later—and left behind a wake of exhilarating memories for many diners—Jarr and Antonitsas partnered to open JarrBar in 2015, a tiny slice of a space on the west slope of Pike Place Market with a focus on casual drinks and bar snacks by way of preserved seafood. In 2018, Antonitsas and Jarr opened a legitimate full-service restaurant.

Little Fish helped ring in the Pike Place Market expansion as Seattle's first modern-day craft cannery and restaurant. Antonitsas, who grew up with a Greek father known to stock the pantry with olive oil and tzatziki and a mother who mastered the art of minimalist cooking, shares the Alice Waters mentality of letting ingredients speak first, then doing what you can to help them shine. "The flavor profiles and ingredients are influenced by the Mediterranean," says Antonitsas. "Lots of vegetables and bright, strong flavors such as lemon, anchovies, and olives. Sometimes when I have a perfect ingredient, like an heirloom tomato, a rib-eye steak, or a fresh pasta, instead of finishing with just sea salt, I use a really good quality salt-cured anchovy." Those sorts of savory flavors have earned Antonitsas a new set of devotees at every turn of her career.

1 cup extra-virgin olive oil,
    plus extra for drizzling
2 small yellow onions,
    chopped (roughly 2 cups)
7 cloves garlic
1½ to 2 Tbsp kosher salt
3½ cups yellow split peas
6 cups water or light
    vegetable stock, plus
    more if needed
2 Tbsp freshly squeezed
    lemon juice

Chopped red onion,
    to serve
Chopped fresh Italian
    parsley, to serve

Fava Santorini

SERVES 8 TO 10

Not to be mistaken for fava beans, this yellow dip is from the island of Santorini and made with yellow split peas. It's like hummus, but lighter and with a distinct flavor.

Heat oil in a heavy-bottomed saucepan over medium-high heat, add onion, garlic, and salt, and cook for about 10 minutes, until translucent and lightly golden brown. Add peas and enough water (or stock) to cover them by ½ inch. Stir well. Bring to a simmer, reduce to medium-low heat, and cook for 20 to 30 minutes. Stir frequently to prevent bottom from scalding.

Remove lid and cook uncovered for another 5 minutes, or until peas are soft and excess water is reduced. The consistency should be like refried beans, soft but not runny. Remove from the heat and transfer, in batches, to a blender. Purée until smooth like hummus. (The consistency will thicken as it cools.) Add lemon juice and season with salt.

PLATING Serve at room temperature or just warm, topped with chopped onion, parsley, and a drizzle of oil. Eat it as part of a meze platter with olives, tinned foods such as sardines or octopus, and crusty bread. (Alternatively, serve it with grilled fish or octopus as a main course.)

2 red onions, finely
  chopped
2 cloves garlic, finely
  chopped
½ cup feta, crumbled
3 extra-large eggs
½ tsp ground cinnamon
2 tsp ground cumin
1 Tbsp Aleppo pepper
  or red pepper flakes
Zest and juice of 2 lemons
2 Tbsp kosher salt

2 Tbsp freshly ground
  black pepper
2 cups cooked
  bulgur wheat
½ cup chopped fresh
  Italian parsley
¼ cup chopped fresh dill,
  plus extra for garnish
¼ cup chopped fresh mint
1 cup dried currants
  (optional)

1 cup toasted pistachios
  (optional)
4 lbs ground salmon
  or any seasonal fish
Tzatziki sauce, to serve
Greek salad, to serve
1 tsp olive oil, for drizzling
Edible flowers, for garnish
  (optional)

Salmon and Bulgur Meatballs   SERVES 8 TO 10

Instead of salmon, rock-fish or cod can also be used in this recipe. You can either ask your fishmonger to grind it for you or do it at home. Simply chop the fish, freeze for 20 minutes, and then pulse in a food processor to a ground meat–like consistency.

Preheat oven to 400°F. Line a baking sheet with parchment paper.

Combine all ingredients except fish and accompaniments in a large bowl and mix well. Add fish and mix until just combined. Shape mixture into golf ball–sized meatballs (about ¼ cup each) and place on the prepared baking sheet. (Do not overcrowd, or the meatballs will not brown properly.) Bake for 20 to 25 minutes, rotating once, until meatballs caramelize and the internal temperature reaches 145°F (be careful not to overcook). Increase oven temperature to broil and cook for another 5 minutes until browned.

PLATING Serve the meatballs with tzatziki sauce and Greek salad. Drizzle lightly with olive oil, and garnish with dill and edible flowers, if using.

Mamnoon Carrie Mashaney

CARRIE MASHANEY has spent most of her career cooking Italian food. Since moving to Seattle from Iowa in 1998, she's worked at Cafe Juanita, the much-lamented Beato, Dinette, and Spinasse, where she rejoined her friend Jason Stratton (page 102) and cut her teeth as a chef. "There's a huge part of me that's in that cuisine, for sure," says Mashaney, who has taken a professional 180 in becoming the executive chef of Mamnoon, a traditional Middle Eastern restaurant hinged on the belief that through breaking bread together, barriers and prejudices are broken too.

A tireless pupil of her newfound cuisine, Mashaney travels to Beirut with owners Wassef and Racha Haroun to research and absorb all she can about Mamnoon's deeply rooted culinary traditions. Striking that balance between preserving classic recipes and satisfying her creativity is something Mashaney is learning how to master. "The *shish taouk*, a chicken

dish that's marinated in yogurt, is our bread and butter," Mashaney says. "I always ask myself how we can make it more interesting, so we often play around with the components and the sides."

Mashaney has an appreciation for tradition and well-cooked food, no matter how plain and simple. And because Italian food has played a huge role in shaping her career, her desire to cook that cuisine has not been permanently quelled. "I've probably wasted too much time trying to figure out how to put pasta onto the menu [at Mamnoon]!" she says. I'm trying! Believe me!"

3 large red beets (about the size of baseballs, roughly 1½ lbs total)

¼ cup plus 2 tsp kosher salt (divided)

¾ cup full-fat yogurt

¼ cup tahini

2 cloves garlic, finely grated

3 Tbsp freshly squeezed lemon juice

10 to 12 fresh mint leaves, torn

Warm pita, to serve

Shamandar

SERVES 6 TO 8

This simple, colorful beet salad makes a wonderful accompaniment to meze spreads. It can also be made a day ahead.

In a large saucepan, combine beets, ¼ cup of salt, and enough water to cover and boil for 30 to 40 minutes, until tender. Drain beets and set aside to cool. Rub off skins with your hands, then rinse under cold running water to cool completely. Using a box grater, coarsely grate beets into a bowl.

In a separate large bowl, combine yogurt, tahini, garlic, lemon juice, and the remaining 2 teaspoons of salt. Fold in grated beets. Adjust seasoning to taste.

Spoon into a bowl and garnish with mint leaves. Serve with pita.

AB DOOGH KHIAR

4 cups full-fat yogurt

1½ cups finely chopped Persian or English cucumber

½ cup golden raisins

½ cup crushed walnuts, plus extra for garnish

1 clove garlic, finely chopped

2¼ cups ice water

⅓ cup verjus blanc (we use Fusion brand)

1 Tbsp sherry vinegar

2 tsp rose water

3 Tbsp finely chopped fresh mint

3 Tbsp finely chopped fresh dill, plus extra for garnish

3 Tbsp finely chopped fresh chives

3 Tbsp finely chopped fresh tarragon

2 tsp salt

½ tsp paprika

GARLIC BREAD

Extra-virgin olive oil, for brushing

6 to 8 slices of crusty bread, cut into 1-inch-thick slices

1 clove garlic, peeled and halved

GARNISH

2 to 3 Tbsp ground sumac

1 to 2 Tbsp dried rose petals (optional)

¼ cup extra-virgin olive oil

Ab Doogh Khiar
(Chilled Persian Yogurt Soup)

SERVES 6 TO 8

This light and refreshing, yet substantial, soup is best eaten on hot days. It can be prepared a day ahead of time and kept chilled in the fridge for up to three days until ready to serve.

AB DOOGH KHIAR In a large bowl, combine the soup ingredients and whisk. Season with salt and adjust to taste.

GARLIC BREAD Preheat broiler or grill to medium-high heat.

Brush oil over bread and broil or grill until brown. Transfer to a plate and rub each piece of bread with garlic.

ASSEMBLY To serve, ladle soup into bowls, garnish with sumac, walnuts, dill, crushed dried rose petals, if using, and a drizzle of olive oil. Serve with garlic bread.

Manu's Bodega Manu Alfau

ESCHEWING THE traditional flavors of the Pacific Northwest cuisine he had been cooking for nearly a decade, Manu Alfau took a chance in 2014 by opening Manu's Bodega—a cubby hole in Pioneer Square. The space had sat vacant for years because of its challenging, off-the-beaten-path locale, but the tiny restaurant—best described as a brick-and-mortar version of a giant tropical hug—is big on personality. The yellow and teal space is high on the likability scale, a bit like Alfau himself. "The second I saw it, I knew it was the spot," he says.

Manu's Bodega serves up mean Latin American comfort food, and the city instantly fell in love with signature dishes including its *puerco asado*—a "messy in a good way" slow-roasted pork sandwich topped with house aioli, shredded cabbage, pickled red onion, and chimichurri. And nobody else—not locally, at least—is making handmade gluten-free empanadas

with yucca root. Even the basics—rice and beans, root vegetables, yucca, plantains, pork, and chicken—are notably bold, generously seasoned, and satisfying. Alfau has created a menu that celebrates his Dominican heritage and leans on his classic training in Spanish cuisine and the roots of Latin American food.

The restaurant has even spawned a nearby sibling. Manu's Tacos, a guisado-style taco stand (think stews and braised dishes), is located inside Flatstick Pub with the same "small but mighty" mentality. A former cook of Ethan Stowell (page 188), Alfau continues to work to a high standard of quality and service when it comes to his food—he just uses different vessels.

→ Mi Paella

2 lbs bone-in chicken, in pieces (wings work well)

3 Tbsp salt (divided)

1 Tbsp plus ¼ tsp smoked paprika (divided)

¼ cup olive oil (divided)

1 lb shrimp, with shells

2 qts (8 cups) chicken stock

1 bay leaf

½ link Spanish chorizo (we prefer Palacios), diced

1 Spanish onion, finely chopped

3 cloves garlic, chopped

1 (1-inch) piece ginger, finely chopped

2 California chiles, finely chopped

½ cup Spanish olives, such as Manzanilla, pitted and sliced

4 cups jasmine rice

¼ cup tomato paste

½ cup dry white wine

1 lb clams, cleaned

1 cup English peas

½ cup chopped fresh cilantro, for garnish

1 lime, cut into wedges, to serve

Mi Paella

SERVES 6 TO 8

Locrio—a simple rice dish not unlike paella—is quintessential peasant food in the Dominican Republic and eaten in every household.

Place the chicken in a bowl, season with 2½ tablespoons salt, 1 tablespoon smoked paprika, and 1 tablespoon olive oil. Mix well and set aside at room temperature for 30 minutes.

In another bowl, combine shrimp, 1½ teaspoons salt, ¼ teaspoon smoked paprika, and 1 tablespoon olive oil and mix well. Refrigerate.

In large saucepan, heat stock and bay leaf over medium heat and simmer.

Heat remaining 2 tablespoons oil in a 12-inch diameter paella pan or skillet over medium heat. Add chicken and brown for 3 minutes on each side until golden brown. Transfer to a bowl.

Add chorizo to paella pan and sauté for 2 to 3 minutes. Add onions, garlic, and ginger and sauté for 10 minutes. Stir in chiles and olives and cook for another 8 to 9 minutes, until all the moisture has evaporated. Stir in rice and mix well.

Add tomato paste and stir for 2 minutes, until paste is caramelized. Season generously with salt and increase the heat to high.

Pour in wine to deglaze the paella pan, using a wooden spoon to scrape any bits stuck to the bottom. Pour in the hot chicken stock and bay leaf and shake the pan to distribute everything evenly.

Place chicken in the paella and bring to a boil. Reduce heat to medium-low, cover, and simmer for 10 minutes. Meanwhile, remove the shrimp from the fridge and let stand at room temperature for 5 to 10 minutes. Arrange clams, hinges facing down, in the pan and add shrimp and peas. Cover again and cook for another 12 minutes, until clams open. (Remove any clams that have not fully opened.) Discard bay leaf. Remove from heat and set aside to rest for 10 minutes.

To serve, present the large paella pan to the table and scoop paella from the pan into individual plates or bowls. Make sure to scrape the bottom of the pan for some of that crunchy, satisfying rice crust! Garnish with cilantro and serve with lime wedges.

1 (2-lb) high-quality rockfish fillet, cut into ½-inch cubes

1½ Tbsp fish sauce

1 chayote, green apple, jicama, or cucumber, finely chopped

1 red onion, finely chopped

1 red bell pepper, finely chopped

1 clove garlic, finely chopped

10 fresh sprigs cilantro, stems cut into ½-inch segments and leaves reserved for garnish

1 Tbsp Korean chili flakes

Juice of 2 lemons

Juice of 2 limes

Sea salt

Saltine crackers, to serve

GARNISH

Fresh cilantro leaves

4 radishes, thinly sliced on a mandoline

1 lime, sliced into thin rounds

Shilgochu (shredded Korean chili threads)

Rockfish Ceviche

SERVES 6 TO 8

This refreshing appetizer gets a hint of texture with chayote (a crisp vegetable that resembles a squashed green pear) and Korean chili flakes, which are commonly used to make kimchi. They can be found at Latin or Asian supermarkets.

Put fish and fish sauce into a large bowl, toss, and set aside for 2 to 3 minutes to marinate. Add chayote, onion, bell pepper, garlic, cilantro stems, and chili flakes and use a slotted spoon to fold. Pour in the lemon and lime juice and mix well. Season with salt to taste.

If you are not comfortable eating fish that is slightly pink in the center, the ceviche can be left to marinate for another 10 to 20 minutes in the fridge. Just be sure to strain the marinade afterwards to prevent fish from cooking further.

Reserve marinade for serving.

ASSEMBLY Using a slotted spoon, spoon mixture onto individual plates or a serving platter. Using the back of the spoon, level off the surface so that all the components are visible on the plate.

Garnish with a small spoonful of marinade, cilantro leaves, radishes, 3 to 4 lime slices, and shredded chili threads. Serve with a basket of saltine crackers.

Marmite Bruce Naftaly

IT'S DIFFICULT to sum up the expansive, synchronistic culinary career of Bruce Naftaly, the man who has been widely considered "the father of Northwest cuisine." The truncated version is that he was once head chef of Rosellini's Other Place—a world-class restaurant that sourced local organic ingredients before farm-to-table was even a trend. He went on to open Les Copains in Wallingford, a restaurant that was way ahead of food trends ("What's charcuterie?"—Seattle, 1980), then became executive chef at the Alexis Hotel.

Things really hit a stride in 1985 when Naftaly took over a small pasta shop located on the fringe of Ballard and turned it into an upscale French restaurant. Le Gourmand borrowed aspects of Other Place, from the white tablecloth to a preferred four-night-a-week dinner service schedule. After nearly 30 years and 80-hour work weeks, Naftaly and his wife, Sara,

sold Le Gourmand only to take up residence a few years later in Chophouse Row. The couple acquired the former Chop Shop space and rebranded it Marmite (the French word for "cooking pot").

The relaxed and airy space offers a new playground for familiar dishes served with brilliant stocks and sauces. Fans of Le Gourmand will recognize classic dishes such as the grilled asparagus with Naftaly's intensely flavored morel sauce. And his *sauce vin blanc*—an elixir made with reduced fish stock, white wine, and cream—must be one of the best things to eat in the world. His recipe for longevity is just as simple: "I do what I do, and hopefully, enough people will like it."

CHIVE-BUTTER SAUCE

¼ cup (½ stick) unsalted butter

1½ cups heavy cream

2 Tbsp finely chopped fresh chives

1 Tbsp finely chopped shallots

1 tsp freshly squeezed lemon juice

Salt, to taste

CREPE

½ cup heavy cream

½ cup milk

1 cup unbleached white flour, sifted

4 eggs

⅛ tsp sea salt

1 Tbsp unsalted butter, melted (divided)

BLINTZES

½ cup Kurtwood Farms' Flora's Cheese or farmer's cheese

¼ cup cream cheese or crème fraîche

Butter, for greasing

8 crepes (see here)

Chopped fresh chives or chive blossoms, for garnish

Savory Blintzes with Kurt's "Flora's Cheese" and Chive-Butter Sauce

SERVES 4

This savory blintz dish showcases an incredible cheese made by Kurt Timmermeister, who works next door in Chophouse Row. "The unconventional sauce could be far more complicated, but this is it," says chef Bruce Naftaly. "Secret's out!"

CHIVE-BUTTER SAUCE Combine all ingredients except salt in a heavy-bottomed saucepan and bring to a boil over high heat. Reduce to medium heat and simmer for 15 minutes, until it's reduced to a third and coats the back of a spoon. Salt to taste and set aside.

CREPE Combine all ingredients except butter in a blender and blend until batter just turns smooth. (If you blend too long, too much air will be incorporated into it.) If needed, strain through a fine-mesh strainer.

Brush melted butter in a crepe or sauté pan set over medium heat. Pour in 2 tablespoons batter, tilt pan to spread evenly, and cook for 45 seconds, until solidified and golden brown. Turn over and cook for another 15 seconds. Transfer crepe to a plate and repeat until all batter is cooked.

BLINTZES Preheat oven to 450°F.

Combine cheese and cream cheese (or crème fraîche) in a small bowl and mix well. Grease a baking sheet.

Place a crepe on a work surface and spoon 1 tablespoon of the cheese mixture onto the crepe, slightly off center and closer to you. Fold the sides over and then roll it away from you to create a little square pillow. Repeat to make 8 blintzes.

Arrange blintzes in one layer on the prepared baking sheet and bake for 15 minutes, or until slightly puffed and lightly golden brown.

PLATING Put two blintzes onto each plate, drizzle over the chive-butter sauce, and garnish with chives (or chive blossoms). Serve immediately.

RADISH GREEN PESTO

¼ lb radish greens

1 Tbsp toasted pine nuts

2 cloves garlic

¼ cup extra-virgin olive oil, plus extra for drizzling

Salt, to taste

SPRING RADISH SOUP

½ cup (1 stick) unsalted butter

1 yellow onion, finely chopped

2 shallots, finely chopped

1 leek, white part only, washed and finely chopped

1½ lbs red spring radishes, washed and halved, plus extra for garnish

4 cups chicken stock

½ tsp rose water

Salt, to taste

Radish green pesto (see here)

Organic rose petals, unsprayed and fragrant, for garnish

Spring Radish Soup

SERVES 4 TO 6

This springtime dish is earthy and full-flavored with a bit of heat and stunning color. To add a toasty flavor to the soup, roast half of the radishes in a 400°F oven for 15 minutes until lightly golden brown.

RADISH GREEN PESTO Combine ingredients in a blender and purée until smooth.

SPRING RADISH SOUP Melt butter in a nonreactive, heavy-bottomed skillet over low heat. Add onion, shallot, and leek and sauté for 20 minutes, until softened and translucent. Add radishes and stock and bring to a boil over high heat. Reduce heat to medium-low and simmer, covered, for 8 to 10 minutes, or until radishes have softened.

Transfer mixture, in batches if necessary, to a blender and purée until smooth. Add rose water and season with salt (it brings out the savory flavor from the stock).

PLATING Pour soup into bowls, garnish with a dollop of radish green pesto, sliced radishes, and rose petals. Drizzle oil over soup and serve.

Marseille Brandin Myett & Liz Pachaud

INDUSTRY COLLEAGUES Brandin Myett and Liz Pachaud opened Honor Society Coffee in Melrose Market in 2016, initially utilizing the Sitka & Spruce bar in the mornings and afternoons until they eventually coveted the adjoining space—the former Bar Ferd'nand bottleshop. From there, expanding in both size and concept, they rebranded the venture as Marseille.

This chic luncheonette and wine bar seems to check all the artisanal boxes. It serves hearty plant-based foods and small-batch, house-roasted coffee. A thoughtfully curated list of natural wines by the glass and bottle keeps in spirit with its predecessor. It's also a marketplace for locally produced goods: think quality olive oils, spices, cures and preserves. And at the heart of Marseille is a dedication to home-grown foods: spring vegetable terrine made with Vashon Island produce; almond-date granola with incredible house-made cashew milk (the default creamer here); and vibrant pastas and salads that speak to the Pacific Northwest.

Most customers don't seem to care that Marseille's menu is mostly plant-based, nor do they notice. And that suits Pachaud and Myett. Whether customers detect what's in their food or not, it's about Marseille fulfilling its promise to the community: "We offer our guests something that is nourishing on multiple levels: aesthetically, literally, in terms of the food we want to offer people, and culturally," says Pachaud. "Without that, none of this even matters."

TARRAGON SALSA VERDE

5 sprigs fresh tarragon, leaves only

1 bunch fresh Italian parsley

Zest of 1 lemon

½ cup extra-virgin olive oil

1 tsp salt

2 Tbsp water

VEGETABLES

½ cup salt (divided)

3 lbs Yukon Gold potatoes

10 high-quality preserved piquillo peppers (we prefer Matiz)

1 large Savoy cabbage, leaves separated

2 lbs asparagus, trimmed

Vegetable oil, for greasing

Sea salt, to taste

GARLIC BROTH

1 head garlic, cloves separated and chopped

8 sprigs fresh tarragon

4 cups water

4 tsp agar powder

Vegetable Terrine with Tarragon Salsa Verde

SERVES 8 TO 12

For this recipe, you'll need a terrine mold or 9- × 5-inch loaf pan, plastic wrap, and cardboard cut to fit the mold. If using a loaf pan, you'll only need 2 pounds potatoes, 1 pound asparagus, and a little over half of the broth.

TARRAGON SALSA VERDE Combine all ingredients in a blender and purée for 45 seconds, until smooth. Set aside.

VEGETABLES Fill a large saucepan with water, add ¼ cup salt, and bring to a boil. Add potatoes and cook for 20 minutes, or until tender but not overcooked. Drain and set aside to cool completely.

Peel potatoes, then cut into thin slices lengthwise to create symmetrical bricks. These will form the sturdy bottom layer of the terrine—if necessary, trim the rounded edges to form rectangles that can fit snugly against each other in the mold.

Insert a knife into the open end of the peppers, slicing through one side to expose the seeds but leaving the pepper intact as one sheet. Remove seeds.

Bring a large saucepan of water to a boil and add 2 tablespoons of salt. Gently lower cabbage leaves into pan and blanch for 3 minutes. Using a slotted spoon, transfer leaves to a bowl of ice water. Drain. Trim the firmer "spines" of the larger leaves, which will help keep the leaves flexible as you press them into the mold.

Bring a large saucepan of water to a boil and add the remaining 2 tablespoons of salt. Gently lower asparagus and blanch for 2 minutes. Using a slotted spoon, transfer spears into a bowl of ice water. Drain and reserve.

GARLIC BROTH Put garlic, tarragon, and water into a saucepan and bring to a boil. Reduce heat to medium-low and simmer for 12 minutes. Strain, return the liquid to the saucepan, and keep at a simmer.

ASSEMBLY In a medium bowl, combine 3 cups of simmering broth with agar powder and whisk until dissolved. (Prepare this at assembly stage to ensure the solution stays fluid—it will set as it cools.)

Lightly oil terrine mold and line with plastic wrap, extending the wrap well beyond edges of the terrine mold. (This step makes it easy to remove the terrine later.)

Line the terrine mold with the cabbage leaves, making sure they overlap and cover all sides. Allow some leaves to hang over the sides—they will eventually cover the entire dish. Season with salt. Ladle in ½ cup warm broth.

Arrange a 1- to 2-inch layer of potatoes in the bottom of the mold, fitting them as snugly as possible. Season with salt. Ladle 1 cup broth over potatoes.

Lay the piquillo peppers on top of the potatoes. Season with salt. Ladle ½ cup broth over peppers. Repeat with asparagus. The broth should coat everything and submerge the ingredients well.

Fold the overhanging cabbage leaves over the top layer, making sure they overlap and cover the terrine.

Cut a piece of cardboard to fit over the top of the terrine. (This will help to press down the terrine while preserving its shape. Wrap cardboard in plastic, place on terrine and top with a weight such as canned vegetables. Refrigerate for at least 12 hours.

Using the ends of the plastic wrap, carefully pull terrine out of the mold and place it on cutting board. Remove plastic. Using a sharp knife, slice terrine widthwise and carefully lay a slice on each plate. Season with sea salt and serve with tarragon salsa verde.

¾ cup chickpea liquid (aquafaba) from homemade or store-bought chickpeas
½ tsp cream of tartar
⅔ cup powdered sugar
1¾ tsp vanilla extract
¼ tsp rose water
Dried hibiscus, crushed, for garnish (optional)

Vanilla Rose Water Meringues

MAKES 20 TO 30 MERINGUES

This recipe is entirely egg-free thanks to the miracle of aquafaba, the reserved liquid from canned or cooked chickpeas. Its delicate texture and neutral flavor allows for the rose water and vanilla to shine without the overly "eggy" flavor of some meringues. This recipe can easily be doubled so feel free to go berserk. If rose water isn't your thing, just omit it and use 2 teaspoons of your favorite extract, such as vanilla, almond, or orange.

Preheat oven to 230°F. Line two baking sheets with parchment paper.

In a bowl, combine aquafaba and cream of tartar and whisk together until dissolved. Transfer mixture to a stand mixer fitted with a whisk attachment and whisk for 15 to 20 minutes on high speed until very stiff peaks have formed.

Add sugar, one tablespoon at a time, and whisk until dissolved. Mixture should appear glossy. Add vanilla and rose water and whisk until mixed.

Using a pastry piping bag fitted with a star tip, portion the meringue into 2-inch rounds on the prepared baking sheets, evenly spacing them 1 inch apart. Bake for 2½ hours, or until firm (do not open the oven door while baking!). Turn oven off and allow meringues to cool completely in the oven.

Transfer meringues to a serving platter and sprinkle with hibiscus, if using. Meringues can be stored in an airtight container in a cool place for up to three days.

Mbar Jason Stratton

JASON STRATTON never imagined his liberal arts degree would bolster his tenure as a chef. It was poetry and printmaking that attracted him to Evergreen State College, but by the time he was contemplating grad school, he was working his way up at Cafe Juanita. It was there that he chose cooking over schooling.

Stratton went on to open Poppy with Jerry Traunfeld (page 126) and Spinasse with Justin Niedermeyer (Stratton later returned as head chef) before taking a stab at his own restaurant, Aragona. But when his bold downtown Spanish concept couldn't quite find its footing, Stratton became a student of Middle Eastern cuisine as the head chef of Mamnoon (page 82). And now, he's found a home with the restaurant's sibling, Mbar.

This rooftop respite sits 14 floors above the city offering breathtaking views of the Space Needle and Lake Union. Plates of food—riffs off classic Levantine

flavor combinations—are shared with groups of people looking for a fun night out. From day one, the runaway dish has been grilled trout spread with caramelized onions—the burnt char is complemented by the cooling richness of labneh and avocado, while za'atar and a little fenugreek butter bring it all together.

It's important to Stratton's inner poet that his food has a point of view, that a story is being told. He "purifies" a dish by looking at a completed course and seeing what he can discard. His style is minimalist and refined, yet rustic—or, as he calls it, "grandma-y." Poetry in motion.

→ Grilled Trout with Labneh, Za'atar, Avocado, and Fenugreek Butter

CARAMELIZED ONIONS
¼ cup olive oil
2 onions, halved through the root, and thinly sliced
Salt, to taste

FENUGREEK BUTTER
2 cups (4 sticks) high-quality unsalted butter
¼ cup dried fenugreek leaves

ASSEMBLY
4 skin-on trout fillets, pinbones removed
Caramelized onions (see here)
2 tsp salt
¼ cup olive oil
1 cup labneh
2 ripe avocados

2 Tbsp high-quality za'atar, plus extra to taste (available at World Spice Merchants, Marx Foods, or online)
Maldon sea salt
Fenugreek butter (see here), melted

Grilled Trout with Labneh, Za'atar, Avocado, and Fenugreek Butter

SERVES 4

Za'atar, a spice blend used throughout the Levant, is made of dried wild thyme, sumac, and sesame.

CARAMELIZED ONIONS Heat oil in a heavy-bottomed skillet over medium-low heat. Add onions and a generous pinch of salt and cook for 1 hour, stirring occasionally, until onions are deeply caramelized but not burnt. (Be sure to scrape the bottom of the pan to release the fond as it caramelizes. If needed, add 1 tablespoon water to prevent burning and to encourage the release of sugars.) Season with salt to taste and set aside.

FENUGREEK BUTTER Melt butter in a saucepan over low heat. Stir in fenugreek leaves and cook for 15 minutes. Remove from heat and set aside for 2 hours, then reheat. Strain butter through a fine-mesh strainer.

ASSEMBLY Set the trout fillets out on a work surface, flesh side up. Spread a quarter of the caramelized onions in a thin, even layer over the flesh side of each fillet. Put two fillets together with the onion sandwiched in between, wrap with plastic wrap, and repeat with the other two. Refrigerate overnight.

Preheat grill to medium-high heat. Preheat oven to 400°F.

Season both flesh and skin sides of each fillet with ¼ tsp of salt and lightly oil the skin side of each trout with 1 Tbsp of oil. Grill trout skin side down for 2 to 3 minutes, until the skin is crisp and the fish is almost cooked through. Rotate fillet 90 degrees and grill for another 2 to 3 minutes. Reassemble trout—skin side out (so they look like two whole fish again)—and transfer to a baking sheet. Roast for 1 to 2 minutes, until flesh turns opaque.

Note: Scrape leftover chilled butter onto a sheet of plastic wrap and roll into a log shape, tying both ends. It can be stored in a tightly sealed container in the fridge for up to a month or in the freezer for six months.

PLATING Divide labneh equally among four serving plates and spread thinly in an arc (if serving on a round plate) using the back of a spoon. Cut each avocado in half lengthwise and remove pits.

Using a spoon, scoop three pieces of avocado onto each plate and arrange around the labneh. Sprinkle 1½ teaspoons of za'atar overtop and season with sea salt. Place a grilled trout fillet over the labneh and drizzle liberally with fenugreek butter. Serve immediately.

½ cup olive oil

3 onions, chopped

8 cloves garlic, thinly sliced

6 bunches collard greens, washed

3 smoked ham hocks

4 dried ñora chiles

2 Tbsp Aleppo pepper (or 1 Tbsp red pepper flakes)

3 cups chicken or pork stock

Salt, to taste

White wine vinegar, to taste

Pauline's Slow-Braised Collard Greens with Ham Hock and Chiles

SERVES 4 TO 6

When chef Jason Stratton was growing up, a version of this dish was always on the table for Thanksgiving and other important family meals. "I loved making this recipe for my mother," says Stratton. "I serve it with a bottle of vinegar on the table so each guest can adjust to their taste." Prepare this dish in advance—you'll see it improve after a day or two in the fridge.

Heat oil a large heavy-bottomed pan over medium-high heat, add onions and garlic, and cook for 2 minutes. Reduce heat to medium-low and cook for another 35 minutes, stirring occasionally with a wooden spoon, until the onions are very soft and translucent, and just starting to get a touch of color.

Strip collards from the thick stems, roll leaves up into thick cigar-like shapes, and slice into 1-inch strips. Add collard greens, ham hocks, chiles, and Aleppo pepper (or red pepper flakes) and cook for another 15 minutes, stirring often, until collards are slightly wilted. Add enough stock to reach halfway up the collards (about 3 cups) and cook, stirring occasionally, for 3 hours, until the collards are very tender and the ham hocks fall off the bone. (There should be an ample amount of rich cooking liquid as the greens cook down. Add more liquid if needed.) Season to taste with salt and vinegar. Serve warm.

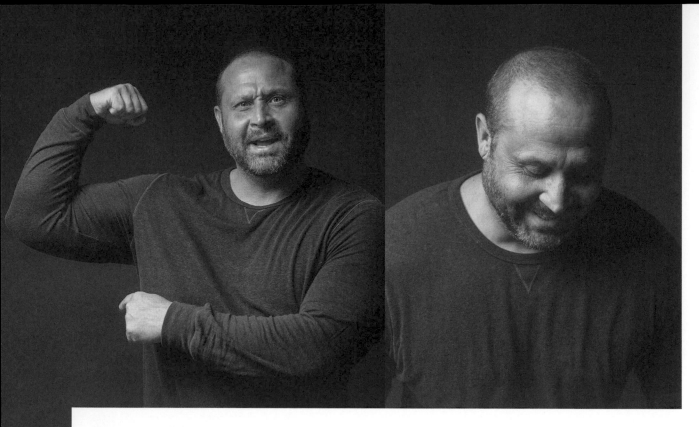

Metropolitan Grill Eric Hellner

THIS CLASSIC steakhouse stands as one of the few remaining stalwarts in Seattle's restaurant landscape. Initially built as an Italian steakhouse in 1983 (would you like a side of fettucine with your rib eye?), this handsome restaurant blossomed into a more modern suitor with a passionate young leader and executive chef named Eric Hellner at the helm.

Obviously Hellner loves steak, but his heart belongs to the dining experience itself. He grew up on Bainbridge Island with a mom who made casseroles, baked pies, and prayed to the church of Betty Crocker. His family always ate at the dinner table and holidays didn't exist unless aunts and uncles brought enough food to feed the entire neighborhood. It's a love so strong he gave up playing hoops in college to work in restaurants, landing his first major role at Elliott's Oyster House in 1989. (He even won a gold medal shucking in the Oyster Olympics. Take that, NBA.)

Today, Hellner is the corporate chef of E3 Restaurants, the mothership that owns Elliott's, Heartwood

Provisions (page 56), and of course The Met. Cooking with heart is a big deal for him and striving for authenticity is a requirement for his kitchen staff. After his decades-long commitment to the industry, he remains as excited today by the power of food as he was when he first started.

And while The Met had a major facelift in 2017, its old soul remains strongly intact. The mahogany tables, brass accents, plush green fabrics, long marble bar and framed photos of celebrity guests (Seinfeld, Clinton, Jordan, and Beckham, to name a few) are what identify this place as a home away from home for many locals and visitors alike. And if we're lucky, it will remain as unabated as Hellner's love of a crowded dinner table.

→ Steak with Southwest Mashed Potatoes, Tomatillo Salsa, and Lime Sour Cream

SOUTHWEST MARINADE

1 cup freshly squeezed
    lime juice

1 cup red wine vinegar

1½ cups brown sugar

½ cup BBQ spice

2 Tbsp ground cumin

2 Tbsp dried sweet basil

2 Tbsp dried Greek oregano

2 Tbsp freshly ground
    black pepper

3 tsp cayenne pepper

SKIRT STEAK

4 (7-oz) skirt steaks

Southwest marinade
    (see here)

1 lime, quartered

4 sprigs fresh cilantro

TOMATILLO SALSA

⅔ cup husked and finely
    chopped tomatillos

⅔ cup red teardrop
    tomatoes, halved

⅔ cup yellow teardrop
    tomatoes, halved

½ cup finely chopped
    sweet yellow onion

2 Tbsp coarsely chopped
    fresh cilantro

2 Tbsp freshly squeezed
    lime juice

2 Tbsp olive oil

1 jalapeño pepper, seeded
    and finely chopped

1 avocado

Steak with Southwest Mashed Potatoes, Tomatillo Salsa, and Lime Sour Cream

SERVES 4

To maximize the flavor of your steak, chef Hellner recommends Snake River Farms' American Wagyu skirt steak due to its higher marbling. This steak can be found at stores such as Tacoma Boys and Metropolitan Market.

SOUTHWEST MARINADE Combine all ingredients in a bowl and mix well. Set aside for 1 hour.

SKIRT STEAK Pour the marinade over the skirt steaks and refrigerate for at least 2 hours.

TOMATILLO SALSA Combine all ingredients except avocado and mix well. Refrigerate for 1 hour. Reserve avocado at room temperature until use.

LIME SOUR CREAM In a small bowl, combine sour cream and lime juice and whisk until well mixed. Refrigerate until serving.

SOUTHWEST MASHED POTATOES Bring a large saucepan of salted water to a boil and add potatoes. Boil for 15 minutes, or until tender. Drain. Return potatoes to pan, add milk and ¼ cup butter, and mash until smooth. Season to taste with salt. Set aside.

Melt remaining 2 tablespoons butter in a skillet over high heat. Add onion, bell peppers, corn, BBQ spice, pepper, and the ⅛ teaspoon salt. Sauté for 2 minutes, or until vegetables are softened. Transfer to a large mixing bowl or pot and stir in mashed potatoes. Keep warm until ready to serve.

LIME SOUR CREAM

1 cup sour cream

6 Tbsp freshly squeezed lime juice

SOUTHWEST MASHED POTATOES

4 yellow potatoes (such as Yukon Gold), coarsely chopped

¼ cup milk

¼ cup (½ stick) plus 2 Tbsp unsalted butter (divided)

⅛ tsp salt, plus extra to taste

¼ cup finely chopped red onion

¼ cup finely chopped red bell pepper

¼ cup finely chopped green bell pepper

½ cup corn kernels

1 Tbsp BBQ spice

⅛ tsp freshly ground black pepper

ASSEMBLY Preheat a charcoal or gas grill to high heat.

Remove skirt steaks from marinade and let excess marinade run off. Grill over medium-high heat for 2 minutes on each side for medium. Transfer to a plate and set aside for 2 minutes to rest.

Peel, pit, and dice avocado and add to salsa. Scoop mashed potatoes onto one side of each plate. Position steaks next to the mashed potatoes and top with salsa. Drizzle lime sour cream over the plate. Garnish with cilantro and lime wedges. Serve immediately.

½ cup (1 stick)
  unsalted butter
6 oz semisweet chocolate
3½ Tbsp cornstarch
¾ cup packed dark brown
  sugar
2 extra-large eggs,
  slightly beaten
¼ cup dark corn syrup

¼ cup Woodford Reserve
  bourbon
4 (5-inch) pastry shells
1½ cups pecan halves
Whipped cream, to serve

Woodford Reserve Bourbon Pecan Tart

SERVES 4

Feel free to use different combinations of chocolate and/or bourbon in this recipe, based on personal preference. Valrhona is a great alternative to use for the semisweet chocolate. Woodford Reserve rye and Masters Maplewood Finish bourbon are recommended alternatives for the bourbon.

Preheat oven to 350°F.

Using a double boiler, melt butter and chocolate together. Set aside to cool.

In a medium bowl, combine cornstarch and sugar and mix well. Stir in eggs and corn syrup until smooth. Add bourbon and melted chocolate mixture and mix well.

Pour this filling into tart shells and top with pecan halves. Place tarts on a baking sheet and bake for 50 minutes, until center of the filling is set. Cool tarts on a rack for 1 hour.

Serve slightly warm or at room temperature with whipped cream.

Nue Chris Cvetkovich

IN JAPANESE folklore, a nue is a supernatural creature that has the body of a tiger, the head of a monkey, and the tail of a snake. Proprietor Chris Cvetkovich, who contributes most of the recipe development to Nue, is also a bit of an enigma. He has no professional cooking experience, but his home kitchen would make any food-science nerd squeal with glee. There's the rotary evaporator (rotavap, for short), a chem lab–looking contraption that extracts flavors from ingredients without the addition of heat. There's the giant refrigerated centrifuge. Oh, and of course, the one item that every modern home-cook has in their possession: a sous-vide machine.

In 2014, Chris took the next step, from gadget geek to full-on restaurateur, after a bout of street food–filled globe-trotting. Just like the food he sampled abroad, the dishes at Nue are simple, flavorful, and creative. So is the decor. There's a large Ekeko doll he hauled back from Lake Titicaca,

advertising posters he ripped down from telephone poles in Mexico City and Saigon, masks from Korea, and farm tools from Romania. Chris continues to seek dish inspiration abroad, but he also finds it in recommendations made by the community of Capitol Hill, where Nue is firmly rooted. In fact, that's how he was introduced to Shark and Bake, a Trinidadian fry-bread sandwich made with fried shark (Nue uses cod) and topped with tamarind and habanero sauces. At any one time, Nue represents no less than a dozen countries on a menu that might see Taiwanese chicken heart poppers sidled up next to grilled Barbadian pig tails. And yet it works.

Chris takes control of the kitchen quarterly for his One World Dinners series—a celebration of cuisines from unrepresented countries such as Syria, Trinidad and Tobago, and Burma. It's like an accessible trip around the world—minus the bad passport photo.

DRESSING

½ cup freshly squeezed lime juice

¼ cup honey

1½ Tbsp Dijon mustard

1 Tbsp freshly ground black pepper

2 tsp granulated garlic

2 tsp ground cumin

2 tsp pomegranate molasses

2 tsp kosher salt

½ cup extra-virgin olive oil

SALAD

¼ cup sliced almonds

¼ cup pitted dates, frozen for 1 hour

1 large bunch young kale, stems and center ribs removed, coarsely chopped (see Note)

2 large carrots, cut into ⅛-inch-thick matchsticks

1 cup crumbled feta

Nigella seeds, for garnish

Note: Young kale works best for this salad. If the leaves are stiff, massage them with a bit of olive oil, a squeeze of lemon juice, and a pinch of salt. Not only does this tenderize the leaves, but it also adds an extra burst of flavor to the dish.

Syrian Kale and Carrot Salad with Shattered Dates

SERVES 2 TO 4

Sweet and savory, textured and bright, this refreshing and hearty dish is quintessentially Syrian. Sticky dates can be difficult to cut. At Nue, they freeze the dates solid using liquid nitrogen and then shatter them in a food processor, but this recipe offers a simpler solution for cutting them at home.

DRESSING Combine all ingredients except the oil in a blender and mix well. With the blender running, gradually add the oil and blend until emulsified. Set aside.

SALAD Preheat oven to 400°F.

Bring a small saucepan of water to a boil. Add almonds and blanch for 30 seconds. Drain and set aside to cool. Transfer almonds to a baking sheet, spread out in a single layer, and toast for 3 to 4 minutes until golden brown. Set aside.

Coarsely chop frozen dates. Put kale, carrots, and dates into a large bowl and toss.

Add dressing and toss again.

Transfer to a serving plate (or individual plates) and top with feta, almonds, and nigella seeds.

GARAM MASALA

1 (1-inch) cinnamon stick, broken into several pieces (to make grinding easier)
2 Tbsp coriander seeds
1 Tbsp cumin seeds
1 Tbsp cardamom seeds
1 Tbsp whole black peppercorns
1 tsp fennel seeds
1 tsp mustard seeds
½ tsp whole cloves
½ tsp red pepper flakes
1½ tsp ground turmeric
¼ tsp freshly grated nutmeg

BUNNY CHOW

¼ cup canola oil
1 onion, chopped (about 1¼ cups)
1 star anise
1 cinnamon stick, whole
6 green cardamom pods
½ tsp fennel seeds
½ tsp cumin seeds
3 Tbsp garam masala (see here)
2 tsp ground turmeric
2 tsp hot paprika
2 tsp ground cinnamon
2 tsp red pepper flakes

1 tsp ground coriander
1 (20-oz) can diced tomatoes
1½ lbs boneless, skinless chicken breast, cut into 1-inch chunks
4 cloves garlic, finely chopped
1½ tsp ground ginger
6 fresh curry leaves
¾ cup water
½ cup heavy cream
5 Tbsp (½ stick plus 1 Tbsp) unsalted butter

2 Tbsp brown sugar
1 Tbsp freshly squeezed lime juice
4 tsp kosher salt
1 pullman loaf or any medium-firm white bread
Chopped fresh cilantro, for garnish
Lime zest, for garnish

South African Bunny Chow

SERVES 4 TO 6

Bunny chow is a popular type of street food in South Africa. A loaf of bread is hollowed out and filled with a meat- or vegetable-based curry. Oh, and it's absolutely delicious.

GARAM MASALA Combine cinnamon stick, coriander seeds, cumin seeds, cardamom seeds, peppercorns, fennel seeds, mustard seeds, cloves, and red pepper flakes in a small skillet over medium-low heat. Toast for 2 minutes, or until fragrant. Grind the toasted spices in a spice or coffee grinder to a fine powder. Add turmeric and nutmeg and mix well. (This spice blend can be stored in a sealed jar for up to a month.)

BUNNY CHOW Heat oil in a large sauté pan over medium heat. Add onion, star anise, cinnamon stick, cardamom pods, fennel seeds, and cumin seeds and sauté for 4 minutes, until onion is softened. Add garam masala, turmeric, paprika, cinnamon, red pepper flakes, and coriander. Increase heat to high and fry, stirring often, until spices begin to stick to the bottom of the pan.

Add tomatoes and stir until the juices loosen the spices from bottom of the pan. Add chicken, garlic, ginger, curry leaves, and water and reduce heat to low. Simmer for 10 minutes, or until chicken is fully cooked. Remove cinnamon stick. (Cardamom pods and star anise can also be removed.)

Add cream, butter, brown sugar, and lime juice. Season with salt, to taste. If not serving immediately, refrigerate overnight to meld flavors.

Preheat oven to 400°F. Cut the pullman loaf into 3-inch slices. Place slices on a baking sheet and toast in the oven for 3 minutes.

PLATING Scoop out enough bread to create a "plug" and a bowl from the bread. Ladle curry into the cavity and generously over the sides. Top with bread plug, cilantro, and lime zest.

Oddfellows Cafe + Bar Myles Burroughs

MYLES BURROUGHS makes the kind of cocktails you need to restrain yourself from devouring in a single gulp. His seasonal sips make you crave the bounties of spring and summer and cold-weather drinks in the fall and winter. So it may come as a surprise that Burroughs, The Derschang Group's beverage director, actually started his journey with a focus on wine. Ironically, it was during his time at RN74—a restaurant renowned for its impeccable wine list—that he discovered a passion for cocktails, thanks to bar manager Amanda Reed (Heartwood Provisions, page 56).

Burroughs creates cocktails that tell his story without the rigid tasting rules or ruthless evaluation he'd become accustomed to with wine. And there is some crossover: his calling card is adding wine to cocktails, emphasizing his appreciation for natural winemaking as a way to capture a time and place, and to introduce another layer of acidity to drinks.

He skillfully infuses flavors into existing ingredients rather than taking the kitchen sink approach. For example, his Peas and Q's is a concoction of strawberry-infused pisco, pea-vine syrup, and wine (vermouth and bubbles). For Burroughs, the secret to timeless drinks is simplicity—anything is possible if you can master a three-ingredient cocktail. And that's really the secret to Oddfellows as well: it's seasonally inspired, locally focused, and creatively driven. The ethos here is "simple, lovely food." And Burroughs approaches his drinks accordingly, with as much emphasis on the process as the end result.

→ The Country Doctor and Peas and Q's

HONEY SYRUP

1 cup wildflower honey

1 cup hot water

THE COUNTRY DOCTOR

1½ oz blended scotch
    whisky (we prefer
    Pig's Nose)

1 oz freshly squeezed
    lemon juice

1 oz honey syrup (see here)

3 thin slices peeled ginger

5 to 10 fresh tarragon
    leaves

½ oz Del Maguey Vida
    mezcal (see Note)

Dried fruit slices, for
    garnish (optional)

*Note: If you're new to mezcal
or squeamish about the
smokiness, start with less.
Remember: you can always
add more but you can't take
it away!*

The Country Doctor

SERVES 1

The Country Doctor is
a great introduction to
the lighter side of scotch
and highlights the deep
herbaceous flavors
sometimes lost in the
smoke of mezcal. "It's a
playful nod to both the
classic Penicillin cocktail
from which this drink is
derived," explains Myles
Burroughs, "and to our
community health clinic
up the street."

HONEY SYRUP Combine honey and water in a small bowl, stirring until incorporated. (Syrup can be stored in an airtight container for up to two weeks.)

THE COUNTRY DOCTOR Combine scotch, lemon juice, honey syrup, and ginger in a shaker tin, add ice, and shake. Strain through a fine-mesh strainer into a large rocks glass. Add tarragon to the glass and fill with fresh ice. Top with a ½-ounce float of mezcal and serve with a slice of dried fruit, if using.

PEA VINE SYRUP

1 cup tightly packed
   pea tendrils

2 cups water

2 cups granulated sugar

**STRAWBERRY-INFUSED
PISCO**

1 pint strawberries,
   hulled and halved

1 (750-ml) bottle Campo de
   Encanto Grand & Noble
   pisco

PEAS AND Q'S

¾ oz strawberry-infused
   pisco (see here)

½ oz Carpano Bianco
   vermouth

½ oz pea vine syrup
   (see here)

¾ oz freshly squeezed
   lemon juice

4 oz Brut sparkling wine

Fresh pea tendrils or a
   brandied strawberry,
   for garnish (depending
   on season)

Peas and Q's

SERVES 1

This sophisticated thirst-quencher introduces the well-worn summer staple of strawberry to some unusual companions. The pisco will last for at least a year once strained.

PEA VINE SYRUP In a blender, combine pea tendrils and water and pulse for 1 minute, until incorporated. Alternatively, use an immersion blender. (Blend in short cycles to minimize heat and prevent cooking or oxidation.)

Add sugar and pulse again for another minute. Strain through a fine-mesh strainer and refrigerate syrup until needed. (Syrup can be refrigerated in an airtight container for up to a week.)

STRAWBERRY-INFUSED PISCO Combine strawberries and pisco in a sterile, airtight container and infuse overnight or up to 1 week in a cool, dry place. Strain the berries and return the pisco to the bottle. Strawberries can be frozen and preserved as garnish. (Makes enough for 25 drinks. Leftover pisco can be stored in the fridge, but is best if used right away.)

PEAS AND Q'S Combine pisco, vermouth, syrup, and lemon juice in a shaker tin. Add ice and shake, then strain through a fine-mesh strainer into a chilled coupe glass. Top with sparkling wine.

Garnish with pea tendrils or a brandied strawberry.

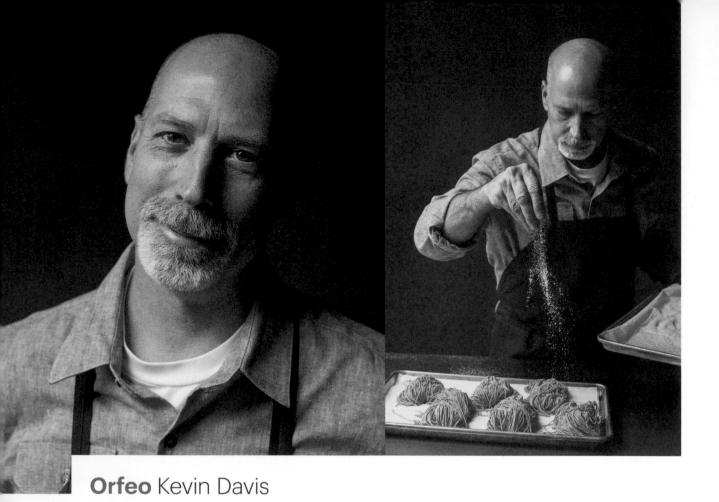

Orfeo Kevin Davis

DUE TO his reputation as a passionate fly fisherman and seafood chef, it came as a surprise to the city's dining community when Kevin Davis opened Orfeo—a Belltown restaurant dedicated to wood-fired cooking and handmade pasta. Unbeknownst to Seattle, Davis had been plotting the concept for decades.

Back in the late nineties, Davis worked at the renowned Tra Vigne in Napa where the chefs were secondary to the kitchen's wood-burning oven and charcoal grill—an approach Davis fell hard for. He finds the artisanal aspect of working with an open flame more rewarding. "While my other restaurants Blueacre and Steelhead Diner are about the ingredients, Orfeo is all about my intention with them." For example, one signature dish sees mussels with garlic, rosemary, lemon, and black pepper roasted over hot coals in the restaurant's unique mesquite charcoal–fired oven. Infused with smokiness and intense heat, the shellfish is steamed in its own juices with the sweet flavors of the ocean still intact.

Orfeo, named after the antagonist in the novel *A Soldier of the Great War* by Mark Helprin, is much more brooding than its siblings—the kind of place where your eyes have to adjust to its darkness after you walk in off the street. And tucked away into the historic Army Building in Belltown, it happens to be more sophisticated and sexier, with its secluded mezzanine dining, long copper-topped bar, and equally winding entryway.

Davis isn't looking to educate his guests or give them something they've never eaten before. He just wants to make people happy by cooking them food they understand, like, and enjoy.

12 oz very fresh large
   mussels, scrubbed and
   debearded
3 Tbsp canola oil
1 Tbsp olive oil
1 Tbsp finely chopped garlic
1 Tbsp finely chopped
   shallots
1 tsp finely chopped
   preserved lemon
1 tsp kosher salt

½ tsp freshly ground
   black pepper
½ tsp chopped fresh
   rosemary
Juice of ½ lemon
½ lemon
Crusty bread, to serve

Roasted Mediterranean Mussels

SERVES 2 TO 4

Orfeo's surprisingly quick-and-easy signature dish allows for endless variations. You'll need three essential things: very fresh large mussels, a charcoal grill, and a 12-inch cast-iron skillet.

Prepare charcoal grill by lighting briquettes. Allow them to burn until completely combusted and red coals remain. (It should be very hot but not flaming.) Place a large cast-iron skillet on top and cover.

In a large bowl, combine all ingredients except the ½ lemon and toss well. Remove skillet from the grill (remember to use an oven mitt!) and, working quickly, place the lemon half, cut side down, in the center of the skillet (it should sizzle). Carefully transfer ingredients from the bowl into the skillet, cover, and cook for 2 to 3 minutes, until mussels are cooked through.

Remove skillet from the grill and squeeze the juice of the roasted ½ lemon over the mussels. Serve immediately in the skillet, along with crusty bread and a side bowl for shells.

CAPELLINI

20 oz "00" flour (we prefer Caputo Pasta Fresca & Gnocchi)

2 cups egg yolks (about 2 dozen)

2 Tbsp extra-virgin olive oil

GRACIE'S CAPELLINI

1 (5-oz) nest capellini (see here), frozen

2 Tbsp high-quality whole butter (we prefer Grand Cru or Plugrá)

1 small clove garlic, finely chopped

½ tsp finely chopped fresh thyme leaves

½ tsp kosher salt, plus extra for pasta water

¼ tsp ground white pepper

½ cup pasta water

1½ tsp high-quality white truffle oil (we like one sold at the Truffle Cafe in Pike Place Market)

¼ cup grated Parmesan, plus extra for garnish

1 cup deep-fried celery or basil leaves, for garnish (optional)

Shaved black truffle, garnish (optional)

Gracie's Capellini

SERVES 2

Named after chef Kevin Davis's daughter, Orfeo's most popular pasta dish is a celebration of the fine art of handmade pasta. Davis likes to use Caputo flour for the pasta dough and finishes the plate with a high-quality truffle oil. This elegant dish may look simple, but the flavor combination is decidedly grown-up. Be sure to make the pasta in advance so you have time to freeze it before preparing the finished dish.

CAPELLINI In a stand mixer fitted with a paddle attachment, mix flour on low speed. Slowly add egg yolks and olive oil, until yolks are incorporated. Switch to the dough hook attachment and knead on speed one for 10 minutes. Wrap in plastic wrap and allow to rest for at least 20 minutes or refrigerate for later use.

Using a rolling pin, flatten dough to a ½-inch thickness. Using #9 on a pasta machine, feed pasta through. Fold it over into a square and crank through again. Change setting to #6 and roll through. Repeat on #4 setting, then #2, until it's thin (but not paper thin). Cut dough into capellini using a pasta cutter (or you can hand cut with a very sharp knife). Weigh out 5-ounce nests and place each one in a separate freezer bag. Pasta nests can be stored in the freezer in individual ziplock bags for at least a month. (Makes seven nests. Each nest will serve two people.)

GRACIE'S CAPELLINI Pour 4 cups of water into a saucepan, add 3 tablespoons kosher salt, and bring to a boil over high heat. Carefully lower in pasta and cook for 2 minutes or until al dente. Drain, reserving ½ cup pasta water.

Meanwhile, melt butter in a skillet over medium heat. Add garlic and render for 1 minute until blond, but not colored. Add thyme, salt, and pepper, then the pasta water.

Add cooked pasta to pan and simmer until most of the liquid has been absorbed. Add truffle oil and Parmesan and remove from heat. Toss until cheese is melted and incorporated.

PLATING Transfer to warm pasta bowls and garnish with Parmesan, celery or basil leaves, and black truffle shavings, if using.

Poppy Jerry Traunfeld

AS THE world turns to eating more whole plant foods and less of everything else, many have become unapologetic fans of chef and garden maven Jerry Traunfeld. "I've always loved plants and gardening," says Traunfeld. "That connection has defined my cooking."

In the eighties, Traunfeld was the chef at the Alexis Hotel and cooked with locally sourced herbs and produce while nurturing relationships with regional farmers. In the nineties, he put The Herbfarm on the map with his seasonal, regional cooking inspired by the restaurant's own kitchen gardens and won an endless string of accolades. Now, with Poppy, the dream restaurant Traunfeld imagined after traveling to India, he's utilizing his extensive urban herb garden and a world of spices to highlight the best ingredients of the Northwest once again.

A devotion to culinary herbs and a focus on flavor have always been at the heart of Traunfeld's cooking, and this commitment has carried through at Poppy. Here it is interpreted on the thali, which is a tray of many dishes served all at once to each guest. For instance, a roast chicken thali is served with garden-driven dishes such as chilled borscht with dill and sour cream; radicchio, Asian pear, and hazelnut salad; minted lentil and goat cheese strudel; zucchini with harissa, basil aioli, and puffed rice; and blackberry pickle. Dining thali-style is a flavor experience.

Named after Traunfeld's mother, Poppy is a bright, airy space that's reminiscent of the Danish-modern aesthetic he grew up with. While the menu is built around thalis and there is a tandoor oven in the kitchen, it is not an Indian restaurant. The cuisine is driven by seasonal ingredients highlighted with herbs and spices, many of which Traunfeld himself tends in the garden (that also happens to be open for seating during warmer months). This translates into dishes such as berry, fresh currant, hazelnut, and sorrel salad or Nooksack River coho salmon with lobster mushrooms, bacon, and red wine sauce. The best part about a thali? Sharing is not an expectation.

2 Tbsp unsalted butter

½ large onion, chopped

3 Tbsp coarsely chopped fresh sage

4 very ripe tomatoes, coarsely chopped (about 3 cups)

1½ cups water

1½ tsp kosher salt

¼ cup heavy cream

¾ cup very ripe strawberries, coarsely chopped

Freshly ground black pepper, to taste

Summer Tomato, Sage, and Strawberry Soup

SERVES 6

Scientifically speaking, tomatoes are fruits and strawberries are not, but their ripe and fragrant flavors harmonize. The herb garden at Poppy has an abundance of fresh sage for most of the year and it adds just the right savory note to this memorable dish.

Melt butter in a large saucepan over medium heat. Add onion and sage and sauté for 4 to 5 minutes, until onion is softened. Add tomatoes, water, and salt. Reduce heat and simmer, covered, for 15 minutes. Remove from heat, stir in the cream and strawberries, and set aside to cool slightly.

Working in batches, transfer soup to a blender and purée until very smooth. To serve, reheat soup and season with pepper to taste.

2 globe eggplants,
  caps trimmed and
  cut lengthwise into
  ¾-inch-thick slices
2 qts (8 cups) cold water
¼ cup kosher salt
2 cups chickpea flour
4 cups canola oil,
  for deep-frying
Buckwheat honey
  (see Note)
Fleur de sel or sel gris

Note: Buckwheat honey has a deep, heady flavor that pairs incredibly well with deep-fried eggplant. If you don't have it on hand, you can substitute chestnut or wildflower honey.

Eggplant Fries with Sea Salt and Buckwheat Honey

SERVES 4 TO 6

Eggplant Fries have been on Poppy's menu since opening day. Inspired by Indian pakoras, they have a lightly crisped outside and a creamy inside. When making them at home, you'll need hungry guests at the ready, as their crispness doesn't last long. A deep fryer is handy for this recipe, but a wok makes a decent alternative. Just be sure to stabilize it with a wok ring or use a flat-bottomed wok on an electric stove.

Cut each eggplant slice widthwise into ¾-inch strips.

Combine water and salt in a large pot and stir until salt dissolves. Add eggplants and soak for 15 minutes.

Put flour into a large shallow bowl.

Pour oil into a deep fryer, wok, or large saucepan and heat over medium heat to a temperature of 350°F.

Using a slotted spoon, transfer half of the eggplant to a strainer and shake to remove excess water. Put the pieces into the flour and turn to coat evenly. Put them back into the strainer and gently shake to remove excess flour. Using tongs, carefully lower eggplant pieces into the hot oil and deep-fry for 4 to 5 minutes, until evenly browned and crisp. Transfer to a plate lined with paper towels to drain.

PLATING Arrange eggplant fries on a plate. Drizzle buckwheat honey overtop and season with a large pinch of sea salt (such as fleur de sel or sel gris). Serve immediately while you repeat the process with the remaining eggplant pieces.

Poquitos Manny Arce

MEXICAN FOOD with a light touch. Many considered this an inauthentic approach when Poquitos first opened in 2011. Where's all the cheese? And cheap tacos? And fatty refried beans? However, chef Emanuel "Manny" Arce believes that when done correctly, Mexican cuisine can be delicate. It's a bold stance from someone who, until then, had never cooked Mexican cuisine professionally.

Previously, Arce had worked at Union, Osteria La Spiga, and Bastille Café & Bar, which would later become a sister restaurant to Poquitos. Time spent in Italy and San Sebastian after culinary school had also informed his preferred culinary style: creating food that is light, bright, acidic, and spicy. And that's the tone he takes at Poquitos.

The Spanish word for "a little bit," Poquitos is anything but. At nearly 3,500 square feet (not

including the covered patio), the place is one big, lively dinner party night after night. Arce offers time-less classics such as the achiote-citrus marinated Yucatán Chicken and the Grilled Summer Vegetable Cazuela—Japanese eggplant, yellow squash, and zucchini finished with garlic oil and smoked jalapeño-cashew crema and served with traditional rice, beans, and tortillas. He's not trying to blow anyone's mind with new techniques or new flavor combinations, saying, "I want to make tasty food that people want to eat and feel good about afterwards." And Poquitos is exactly that: a little bit of goodness in every bite.

5 large mixed heirloom tomatoes (about 2 lbs), cut into wedges and random shapes

2 cups chopped cantaloupe

1 tsp kosher salt, plus extra to taste

½ tsp freshly ground black pepper

3 guajillo chiles, seeded

2 dried chiles de arbol

¾ cup apple cider vinegar

3 Tbsp water

Juice of 1 lime

¼ cup fresh mint leaves, torn (divided)

¼ cup fresh cilantro leaves, coarsely chopped (divided)

¼ cup extra-virgin olive oil

Tomato, Melon, and Chile Salad

SERVES 6

Place the tomatoes and cantaloupe in a bowl, season with salt and pepper to taste, and set aside.

In a blender, combine chiles, vinegar, water, and a generous pinch of salt, and blend until smooth.

Add ½ cup of the chile purée to the bowl of tomatoes and melon, then the lime juice and half the mint and cilantro. Toss gently. Pour in oil and toss again. Season with salt to taste.

Transfer salad to a large serving platter, drizzle it with more chile purée, and scatter remaining mint and cilantro leaves on top. Serve immediately.

SALSA DE CILANTRO Y YERBA BUENA

2 cups fresh cilantro leaves

1 cup fresh Italian parsley leaves

¼ cup pepitas

6 serrano peppers

¼ cup white wine vinegar

¼ cup freshly squeezed lime juice

½ cup olive oil

Salt, to taste

LEG OF LAMB

¼ cup olive oil

10 cloves garlic, thinly sliced

2 Tbsp plus 2 tsp fresh oregano

1 Tbsp fresh thyme leaves

1 boneless leg of lamb, rolled and tied (ask your butcher)

Salt and freshly ground black pepper, to taste

2 limes, one halved, one cut in wedges

¼ cup pepitas

Fresh herbs, such as scallions, cilantro, mint leaves, and Italian parsley, to serve

Grilled Leg of Lamb with Salsa de Cilantro y Yerba Buena

SERVES 6

SALSA DE CILANTRO Y YERBA BUENA Combine all ingredients except the olive oil and salt in a blender and blend on high. With the blender running, gradually add oil and blend until emulsified. Season to taste with salt. Transfer to a small serving bowl and refrigerate until use.

LEG OF LAMB In a small bowl, combine oil, garlic, and herbs and mix well. Rub mixture over lamb, then marinate in airtight container in the refrigerator for at least 12 hours.

Preheat a gas or coal grill to 350°F. Generously season lamb with salt and pepper, put onto the hottest part of the grill, and sear for 5 minutes on each side, rotating 3 to 4 times.

Move lamb to the least hot part of grill, cover, and cook for 30 to 45 minutes. Rotate every 10 to 15 minutes, until the internal temperature reaches 133°F to 138°F and the lamb is medium rare. Transfer the leg of lamb to a cutting board and set aside to rest for 10 to 15 minutes. While the lamb is resting, grill the lime halves for 5 minutes until charred.

PLATING Untie and slice the lamb. Place on a serving platter and serve with salsa de cilantro y yerba buena, pepitas, fresh and grilled limes, and fresh herbs.

Porkchop & Co. Paul Osher

THE MEAT industry has been ingrained in Paul Osher since he was a kid, which comes as no surprise considering his family owned a kosher meatpacking business in Chicago, and he worked at a corner deli while he was attending college. But what makes his story particularly fascinating is that Osher was a vegetarian for 15 years before he discovered an interest not only in cooking, but specifically in curing meats. His eating habits changed entirely, and he dropped out of a UCLA doctoral program to become a chef. Eventually, he moved to Seattle to take over the former Belle Clementine space with his wife, Raquel. (In fact, the first time he ever made pastrami was to impress her.)

Porkchop & Co. may be a whimsical nod to the restaurant's home-cooked vibe, but comfort aside, the food is also smart. Everything from the pork belly hash to the jerk chicken is made from scratch using the best ingredients available. The menu is fun, creative, and more vegetable-focused than most people think (the cauliflower sandwich and smoked beet toasts are big hits). And of all the items on the menu, Osher is proudest of a dish that is a total throwback to his family's business: the beef cheek pastrami sandwich made with grass-fed beef cheeks that are deliciously cured, smoked, and thinly sliced. Satisfying and homey, it reflects Osher's commitment as a restaurateur to serving high-quality food in a casual way. It's important to him that everyone leaves with a full stomach and a smiling face.

2 lbs red beets, peeled

½ cup olive oil

1 cup slivered almonds, toasted

4 cloves garlic

¼ cup sherry vinegar

1 Tbsp honey

Water, as needed

Wood chips, such as applewood, for smoking

6 to 8 slices toast, to serve

Blue cheese, to serve

Arugula, to serve

Maldon sea salt, for garnish

Smoked Beet Spread

SERVES 6 TO 8

This spread is earthy, rich, sweet, and nutty. Beets take to smoke well, but if you don't have a smoker, try roasting them in the oven. It's still delicious without the smokiness.

Preheat oven to 400°F.

Put beets into a small roasting pan. Drizzle them with 1 tablespoon of oil and rub until beets are well coated. Add an inch of water to the pan and cover with foil. (The water steams and cooks the beets before they concentrate from the roasting.) Cook for 1 hour, or until the beets are very tender. Set aside to cool.

Cut beets into ½-inch discs and place them in a smoker. Smoke for 1 hour, until they take on a good amount of smoky flavor (but not so much that they're bitter). Chop them up into cubes.

Put almonds and garlic into a food processor and pulse several times, until coarsely crushed. Add 2 cups beets, sherry vinegar, and honey. Pulse a few more times until well chopped. With the food processor running, drizzle in oil in a steady stream. If it looks too thick (and it often does), add a little water to thin it out.

PLATING Serve this beet spread on toast with blue cheese, arugula, and sea salt.

SPICE MIX

1 tsp caraway seeds

1 tsp fennel seeds

1 bay leaf

1 tsp cumin seeds

1 tsp ancho chili powder

1 tsp smoked paprika

SHAKSHOUKA BASE

2 Tbsp olive oil

½ yellow onion, finely chopped

3 cloves garlic, grated using a microplane

1 (28-oz) can good-quality crushed tomatoes

Handful of kale or chard, chopped

ASSEMBLY

4 eggs

Handful of feta

Fresh cilantro, finely chopped

Fresh Italian parsley, finely chopped

Salt, to taste

4 slices hearty bread, toasted

Shakshouka

SERVES 4

Shakshouka strikes the perfect balance of a hearty meal made with light ingredients. I recommend making a double or triple batch of the spice mix, because it works on just about everything.

SPICE MIX Grind the caraway seeds, fennel seeds, and bay leaf together in a spice grinder. (Alternatively, put them onto a cutting board and break them up with the bottom of a heavy pan.) Add the cumin seeds, chili powder, and smoked paprika.

In a small skillet over medium heat, toast the spice mix for 2 to 3 minutes, until fragrant. (Be careful not to burn it.) Set aside until use.

SHAKSHOUKA BASE Heat oil in a deep ovenproof skillet over medium heat, add onion and garlic, and sauté for 3 to 4 minutes, until translucent. (Reduce heat if they start to brown.) Add spice mix and stir for 1 to 2 minutes, until fragrant. Add tomatoes and cook for 5 minutes, until slightly thickened. Stir in kale (or chard) and cook for another 2 to 3 minutes, until tender.

ASSEMBLY Preheat oven to 400°F.

Use the back of a spoon to push down into the shakshouka base and make a shallow crevice for each egg. Crack an egg into each crevice, place skillet in oven, and cook for 12 minutes, or until egg whites are fully cooked and yolks are still runny.

PLATING To serve, top shakshouka with feta, herbs, and salt to taste and serve immediately—straight out of the pan if you like!—with toasted bread. Any leftover shakshouka can be stored in the fridge for up to a week. It also freezes well!

← Shakshouka (center) and Smoked Beet Spread

Revel Rachel Yang

THE CITY crushed hard on Revel when it opened in Fremont in 2010. The menu was a heady compilation of fusion foods from noodles to rice bowls to savory pancakes topped with pork belly, kimchi, smoked mussels, short rib, or crispy paneer. And it all tasted as good as it sounded. Seattle was hooked, and the adoration hasn't dulled since.

Chef-owners Rachel Yang and Seif Chirchi have been a breath of fresh air since moving to Seattle from New York in 2006, when they arrived to help launch Coupage, the ambitious yet short-lived Korean-French fusion restaurant in Madrona. When the couple branched out on their own the following year with Joule, their reputation skyrocketed. They now have four restaurants under their belt (including Trove and Revelry in Portland), creating inimitable menus for each of them and luring diners with unique and contemporary Korean-inspired food.

Yang and Chirchi often return to the origin of a dish, asking themselves how a line cook from Korea might prepare it. From there, they put their spin on it using pantry items from just about everywhere in the world. We're talking corned lamb, mizuna, and spicy nuoc cham salad; patatas bravas, chipotle, and tomato furikake dumplings; and a lemongrass beef, cilantro noodle, yu choy, and pickled tomato noodle dish. Need I say more?

Former *New York Times* food critic Frank Bruni once described Revel as a contemporary Korean restaurant that's a sleeker, sexier Momofuku Ssäm Bar. But Seattleites are too busy eating to notice the decor.

4 summer squash, assorted,
    cut into ¼-inch half-
    moons
2 Korean chile peppers,
    cut into thin rings
2 shallots, cut into thin rings
1 ear summer corn, kernels
    cut off
4 cups rice vinegar
2 cups water

2 cups granulated sugar
¼ cup Japanese miso
Fresh Thai basil leaves,
    for garnish

Summer Squash Bread and Butter Pickles

SERVES 4 TO 6

In a large sterilized glass jar or plastic container, combine squash, peppers, shallots, and corn.

In a medium saucepan, combine rice vinegar, water, sugar, and miso and bring to a boil over high heat. Boil until sugar and miso dissolve, then pour over zucchini mixture.

Refrigerate for at least 24 hours. To serve, transfer to a bowl and garnish with Thai basil. The pickles can be stored in the fridge for up to one month.

KALUA PORK BELLY

4 to 6 cloves garlic

1 (2-inch) piece ginger, chopped

½ cup sake

1 Tbsp chipotle powder

½ cup Korean bean paste

2 Tbsp Korean chili paste

1 (3-lb) pork belly, skin removed (about a 10- × 6-inch piece)

1 banana leaf, large enough to wrap pork belly

Assorted leaves of greens such as radicchio and Napa cabbage, to serve

KOREAN CHIMICHURRI

1 cup kimchi, finely chopped

½ cup canola oil

2 Tbsp sesame oil

2 Tbsp soy sauce

¼ cup chopped scallions

¼ cup chopped perilla or shiso leaves (you can also substitute basil)

Kalua Pork Belly with Korean Chimichurri

SERVES 4 TO 6

Patience is an unlisted ingredient in this recipe. You'll need to allow 12 hours for the pork belly to marinate.

KALUA PORK BELLY In a blender, combine garlic, ginger, sake, chipotle powder and the pastes and blend until smooth.

Rub marinade over pork belly, then place it on top of the banana leaf and wrap to enclose. Wrap again in foil and refrigerate for 12 hours to marinate.

Preheat oven to 300°F.

Place wrapped pork belly on a baking sheet and roast for 1½ to 2 hours, or until the pork is tender and reaches an internal temperature of 155°F.

KOREAN CHIMICHURRI Combine ingredients in a bowl and mix well.

ASSEMBLY Slice pork belly into ½-inch slices. Serve with Korean chimichurri and lettuce and cabbage leaves for *ssam* (Korean lettuce wraps).

← Kalua Pork Belly with Korean Chimichurri (center) and Summer Squash Bread and Butter Pickles

Rider David Nichols

DAVID NICHOLS has never known anything other than "cooking local." He was raised on a farm in central Washington (with a 300-acre orchard of apples, pears, and cherries), but it wasn't until he went to the International Culinary Center (formerly the French Culinary Institute) in New York City that he realized the enormous possibilities cooking professionally could afford him. He eventually worked around the world. First Italy, then Turks and Caicos (where he snorkeled to work, no joke), and Australia. "I'm drawn to flavors," says Nichols. "I love playing around with North African spices like cumin and paprika, discovering flavor profiles from places I've traveled to and people I've worked with."

Located in the Hotel Theodore (formerly the Roosevelt Hotel), this wood-burning, seafood-heavy, market-to-table restaurant is an homage to Teddy Roosevelt's ragtag team of military volunteers

known as the Rough Riders—and is aptly decorated with tufted leather booths, exposed brick, and subway-tiled columns. The open kitchen is a stately playground for Nichols whose back-to-basics approach depends on both simplicity and classic technique. And his roasted carrot pasta is a perfect example. While this dish requires more involvement than most—from roasting the carrots to dehydrating them, turning them into powder and into a dough—it remains relatively simple in preparation.

Nichols's reason for cooking is as uncomplicated as his style: he just likes being a part of people's evenings. Says Nichols, "When people come in to eat, I want to make their time here amazing yet remain approachable."

→ Roasted Carrot Chitarra with Steamed Clams and Chiles

ROASTED CARROT CHITARRA
6 large carrots
2 cups "00" flour
2 tsp ground turmeric
4 eggs

CALABRIAN CHILE BUTTER
½ cup Calabrian chiles (the ones in oil from the store work best, as they are less spicy and have a deeper, richer flavor)
Zest of 2 limes
½ cup (1 stick) unsalted butter, room temperature

Roasted Carrot Chitarra with Steamed Clams and Chiles

SERVES 4

This recipe requires a few specialty items, including a chitarra pasta maker and a dehydrator; however, the pasta can be cut into any shape and carrot powder makes a decent substitute for the dehydrated carrot. "Once you master a simple pasta dough recipe," says chef David Nichols, "you will never go back to dried pasta."

ROASTED CARROT CHITARRA Preheat grill or broiler to high heat. Char carrots for 8 to 10 minutes, until blackened but not burnt. (Once skin starts to blacken on one side, rotate and repeat on other side until a deep brown.) Transfer to a bowl and cover with plastic wrap to steam for 5 minutes.

Peel off blackened skin and coarsely grate carrots using a box grater. Place grated carrot in a 160°F dehydrator for 8 hours. (Alternatively, preheat oven to lowest setting, place carrots on a baking sheet, and bake for 4 hours, stirring occasionally, until dehydrated.)

Transfer dried carrot to a clean coffee grinder and pulse to a powder. In a stand mixer fitted with a dough hook attachment, combine carrot powder, flour, and turmeric and mix on low. Slowly add eggs one at a time until the dough forms a ball. Mix for an additional 5 to 7 minutes until the consistency is firm and smooth. Wrap dough in plastic wrap and refrigerate for 1 hour.

Working in batches, roll out small pieces of dough into ⅛-inch-thick sheets and place on the chitarra pasta maker. Using a rolling pin, slowly roll the pin back and forth over the dough until the dough is cut. (Alternatively, use a linguini or spaghetti attachment on any pasta machine, or use a pizza-cutting wheel.) Set aside until needed.

CALABRIAN CHILE BUTTER Using a food processor, process chiles until finely chopped. Add lime zest and butter and blend for 20 seconds or until ingredients come together. Scrape mixture onto a sheet of plastic wrap and roll into a log shape, tying both ends. Refrigerate until needed. (The butter can be made weeks in advance and frozen until use.)

LEMON-HERB BREAD CRUMBS

1 Tbsp extra-virgin olive oil

4 Tbsp panko bread crumbs

Zest of 2 lemons

1 Tbsp chopped fresh chives

1 Tbsp chopped fresh Italian parsley

Salt and freshly ground black pepper, to taste

ASSEMBLY

1 Tbsp salt

1 Tbsp extra-virgin olive oil

1 shallot, sliced

3 cloves garlic, sliced

1 lb Manila clams, cleaned

½ cup dry white wine

1 recipe chitarra pasta (see here)

3 Tbsp Calabrian chile butter (see here)

Juice of 2 limes

Salt and freshly ground black pepper, to taste

2 Tbsp lemon-herb bread crumbs (see here)

¼ cup fresh cilantro leaves

LEMON-HERB BREAD CRUMBS Heat oil in a skillet over medium heat, add bread crumbs, and toast for 1 to 2 minutes, until golden brown. Remove from heat and set aside to cool. Add zest and herbs and mix together. Season with salt and pepper. Set aside until needed.

ASSEMBLY Fill a large pot with water and salt and bring to a boil. Add pasta and cook for 4 minutes, or until al dente. Drain and set aside.

Meanwhile, heat oil in a large skillet over medium-high heat. Add shallot and cook for 5 minutes, until translucent. Add garlic and sauté for another minute, until fragrant and lightly golden brown.

Add clams and wine and steam uncovered for 3 to 4 minutes, until clams have opened. (Discard any clams that have not fully opened.)

Add pasta to skillet and cook for another minute. Stir in Calabrian chile butter and lime juice, then season with salt and pepper.

PLATING Transfer pasta to a large serving bowl. Garnish with lemon-herb bread crumbs and cilantro leaves, and serve.

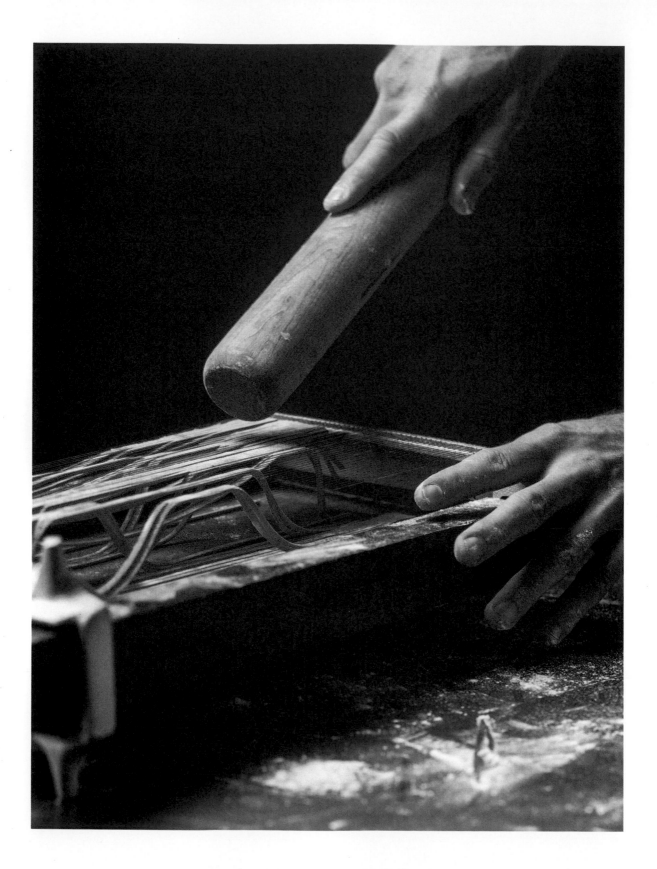

ROASTED WINTER SQUASH
½ winter squash, peeled and
  cut into 1½-inch cubes
1 Tbsp extra-virgin olive oil
1 tsp ground cumin
1 tsp ground paprika
1 tsp fresh thyme leaves
1 tsp Aleppo pepper
Salt and freshly ground
  black pepper, to taste

MINT VINAIGRETTE
1 cup fresh mint leaves,
  thinly sliced
½ cup fresh cilantro leaves,
  chopped
1 shallot, finely chopped
1 tsp red pepper flakes
½ Tbsp Dijon mustard
¼ cup sherry vinegar
½ cup extra-virgin olive oil
Salt and freshly ground
  black pepper, to taste

WHIPPED CHEESE
⅓ cup cream cheese, room
  temperature
¼ cup Greek yogurt
1 tsp ground cumin
1 Tbsp honey
1 tsp freshly ground black
  pepper
2 tsp extra-virgin olive oil
Salt, to taste

TOASTED PEPITAS
2 tsp extra-virgin olive oil
2 Tbsp pepitas
Salt and freshly ground
  black pepper, to taste

ASSEMBLY
1 cup shaved winter squash,
  spiralized
2 kohlrabies, spiralized
¼ cup fresh Italian parsley
  leaves
¼ cup torn fresh mint leaves
  (divided)
¼ cup mint vinaigrette
  (see here)
Salt and freshly ground
  black pepper, to taste
½ cup whipped cheese
  (see here)
1 cup roasted winter squash
  (see here)
2 Tbsp toasted pepitas
  (see here)

Shaved Kohlrabi and Winter Squash with Whipped Cheese

SERVES 4

This standout dish can be prepared with any seasonally available squash. Chef Nichols recommends using a spiralizer to shave the kohlrabi and winter squash, but if you don't have one, cut the vegetables into thin strips or use a peeler to create long ribbons.

ROASTED WINTER SQUASH Preheat oven to 350°F.

In a bowl, combine all the ingredients and toss. Transfer to a baking sheet and roast for 20 to 25 minutes, until tender.

MINT VINAIGRETTE In a mixing bowl, combine mint, cilantro, shallot, and red pepper flakes and mix well. Stir in mustard and vinegar and mix well.

Whisk in oil and blend until emulsified. Season with salt and pepper.

WHIPPED CHEESE In a mixing bowl, combine cream cheese and yogurt and mix. Add remaining ingredients and mix well until incorporated. Set aside.

TOASTED PEPITAS Heat oil in a nonstick skillet over medium-low heat, add pepitas, and toast for 2 to 3 minutes until golden brown. Season with salt and pepper. Transfer pepitas to a plate lined with paper towels.

ASSEMBLY Combine shaved squash and kohlrabi in a large bowl, then add parsley and half the mint. Dress with vinaigrette, season with salt and pepper, and toss.

Spread whipped cheese on a serving platter and place roasted squash on top.

Top with salad, then garnish with remaining mint leaves and pepitas.

RockCreek Eric Donnelly

"**WHAT'S THE** best seafood restaurant in Seattle?" is a question we locals get asked all the time. And in 2013, a new frontrunner was born: RockCreek. Unlike those waterfront restaurants that dish up overpriced fish and chips or clam chowder served in bread bowls, this neighborhood joint in Fremont showcases the kind of innovative sea cuisine our city is capable of. And it's nowhere near the water.

Eric Donnelly wasn't exactly a household name when he opened RockCreek (a nod to the tributary in Montana where he learned to fly fish), but he certainly wasn't new to the game. His seafood education came courtesy of The Oceanaire Seafood Room under Kevin Davis (page 122), whom he replaced when Davis went on to open Steelhead Diner. After eight years at the downtown seafood house, and a few more as the opening chef of Toulouse Petit, he set in motion plans for his own project.

RockCreek is a tribute to Donnelly's "happy place"—a fishing cabin complete with landscape murals, vaulted burlap ceilings, and aged barnwood accents. As a chef, Donnelly aims to hit your palate with lots of flavors and treats every dish like a pH balance—focusing on a few key ingredients that work well together. Take for example the boldly flavored barbecued Alaskan octopus with potatoes, olives, roasted tomato, cannellini beans, and olive aioli, a dish which he personally craves most often.

And while he's still an avid fly fisherman, Donnelly has no interest in opening another seafood restaurant. In fact, in 2016, he opened the meat-centric Flint-Creek, named after the waterway that runs parallel to the one that inspired the name of RockCreek. But if you're craving fresh-as-if-you-caught-it-yourself seafood, the lure of RockCreek's menu will have you hooked.

CANNELLINI BEANS

1 tsp olive oil

1 slice smoked bacon (optional)

½ white onion, coarsely chopped

½ carrot, coarsely chopped

1 rib celery, coarsely chopped

2 sprigs fresh thyme

1 bay leaf

2 cups dried cannellini beans, presoaked

2 qts (8 cups) cold water

2 Tbsp kosher salt

1 Tbsp ground white pepper

OIL-CURED OLIVE AIOLI

½ cup oil-cured olives, pitted

2 Tbsp Spanish sherry vinegar

2 egg yolks

1 clove garlic

1 tsp kosher salt

1 cup grapeseed or canola oil

OVEN-ROASTED TOMATOES

6 ripe San Marzano or Roma tomatoes, halved

¼ cup olive oil

Salt and freshly ground black pepper, to taste

12 slices raw garlic

1 Tbsp chopped fresh thyme

Grilled Octopus Salad

SERVES 4 TO 6

Start this recipe with fresh, raw octopus in the 4- to 6-pound range. They are usually available at reputable fish markets as well as most well-known Asian markets. You'll need a nonreactive stainless steel pot for this recipe, too.

CANNELLINI BEANS Heat oil in a large, stainless steel saucepan over medium heat. Add bacon, if using, and sauté for 5 minutes, until crisp and fat is rendered. Add onion, carrot, and celery and cook for another 4 to 6 minutes, until vegetables begin to caramelize.

Add thyme, bay leaf, and beans. Pour in water and bring to a slow simmer.

(Do not add salt to the water as it will prolong the cooking time.) Cook for 25 to 30 minutes, until beans are tender. Discard bay leaf. Season with salt and pepper. Set saucepan aside to cool down (do not drain beans), then refrigerate until needed.

OIL-CURED OLIVE AIOLI In a food processor, combine olives, vinegar, egg yolks, garlic, and salt and process until the mixture forms a paste. With the motor running, gradually add oil and blend until emulsified. Transfer to a glass jar or plastic container with lid. The aioli can be stored in the fridge for up to two days.

OVEN-ROASTED TOMATOES Preheat oven to 250°F.

In a mixing bowl, combine tomatoes and oil, season with salt and pepper, and toss until tomatoes are well coated. Transfer tomatoes cut side up to a baking sheet, then place a slice of garlic on top of each. Sprinkle thyme over the tomatoes.

Roast tomatoes for 2 hours, until dehydrated and concentrated in flavor. Set aside.

CONTINUED OVERLEAF

**GARLIC-CAPER
BAGNA CAUDA**

¼ cup olive oil

4 cloves garlic,
  finely chopped

1 anchovy fillet,
  finely chopped

2 tsp capers, coarsely
  chopped

1 tsp white balsamic vinegar

OCTOPUS

¾ cup cold water

1 cup white vinegar

3 Tbsp kosher salt

2 Tbsp Old Bay seasoning

1 lime, halved

1 orange, halved

1 jalapeño pepper, halved

1 (4- to 6-lb) fresh or
  previously frozen octopus

1 recipe bagna cauda
  (see here)

GARLIC-CAPER BAGNA CAUDA Heat oil in a small saucepan over medium heat. Add garlic and anchovy and cook for 3 minutes, or until fragrant. Add capers and vinegar, stir, and remove from heat. Transfer to a glass bowl or jar. The bagna cauda can be stored in the fridge for up to two days.

OCTOPUS In a large nonreactive pot, combine water, vinegar, salt, and Old Bay seasoning and mix well. Add lime, orange, and jalapeño. Add octopus and bring to a slow simmer over medium heat. Taste the braising liquid at this point and adjust seasoning to taste.

Cook for 1½ hours, or until octopus is tender and fully cooked. (Cut off a small
piece of tentacle and test for doneness.) Set pot aside to cool, then chill in the fridge for at least 12 hours but preferably overnight. This ensures the braising liquid has fully seasoned the octopus flesh.

Transfer octopus to a cutting board, discarding the braising liquid. Using a sharp knife, separate tentacles from body (the body can be discarded) and slice tentacles into 3- to 4-inch-long pieces.

Put tentacles into a bowl and add bagna cauda. Refrigerate, covered, for 2 to 4 hours.

ASSEMBLY
Braised octopus (see here)
1 tsp cold-pressed olive oil
1 clove garlic, sliced
6 to 8 fresh basil leaves
2 cups prepared cannellini
 beans (see here), drained
1½ cups oven-roasted
 tomatoes (see here)
¼ cup oil-cured olives,
 pitted
½ cup fresh Italian
 parsley leaves
Coarse sea salt and freshly
 ground black pepper,
 to taste
1 cup oil-cured olive aioli
 (see here)
Aleppo pepper, to taste

ASSEMBLY Preheat a grill or cast-iron skillet over high heat.

Add octopus and cook for 4 minutes, or until slightly charred. Transfer to a plate and set aside.

Heat oil in a large skillet over medium-high heat, add garlic, and sauté for 2 minutes, or until toasted and slightly browned. Add basil leaves.

Add cannellini beans and oven-roasted tomatoes and sauté for 1 minute. Add olives and parsley and toss quickly. Immediately remove from heat and season with salt and black pepper.

PLATING Spread olive aioli on a serving platter. Spoon cannellini bean salad on top and scatter with parsley leaves. Arrange octopus on the platter and garnish with a few more parsley leaves, sea salt, and a sprinkle of Aleppo pepper. Serve immediately.

HARISSA

¼ cup honey

¼ cup rose petal harissa
(can be found at specialty
grocers, like DeLaurenti,
or online)

¼ cup white wine vinegar

2 tsp preserved lemon zest,
finely chopped

¼ cup extra-virgin olive oil

1 tsp Dijon mustard

Pinch of salt

Pinch of freshly ground
black pepper

PICKLED SHALLOTS

2 cup champagne vinegar

1 Tbsp granulated sugar

1 Tbsp pickling spice

1 cup shallots, thinly sliced
on a mandoline

DUKKAH SPICE

¼ cup whole hazelnuts

1 tsp sesame seeds

1 tsp ground coriander

1 tsp cumin seeds

1 tsp nigella seeds

2 Tbsp unsweetened
coconut flakes

Sea salt, to taste

Lamb Tartare

SERVES 2 TO 4

HARISSA Heat honey in a small saucepan over medium heat, until caramelized and a dark golden brown. (Do not overcook.)

In a small food processor, combine honey with the rest of the ingredients and purée until smooth. (Alternatively, combine ingredients in
a bowl and use an immersion blender.) Set aside until use.

PICKLED SHALLOTS Combine vinegar, sugar, and pickling spice in a small
saucepan and bring to a boil. Remove from heat and steep for 5 minutes.

Place shallots in a small bowl and strain pickling liquid overtop. Cover
with plastic wrap and chill.

DUKKAH SPICE Combine all ingredients except salt in a small skillet and toast
over low heat for 3 minutes, or until aromatic.

Transfer mixture to a food processor or clean coffee grinder and pulse
slightly until coarsely ground. (Do not overprocess—you want to avoid
turning it into a fine powder). Season to taste with sea salt. Set aside
until use.

NIGELLA CRACKERS

2½ cups whole wheat flour

2½ cups all-purpose flour

2 tsp nigella seeds

2 tsp sesame seeds

1 tsp salt

½ cup warm water

¼ cup grapeseed oil

LAMB TARTARE

1 (8-oz) leg of lamb, finely chopped

¼ cup finely chopped radishes

2 Tbsp finely chopped shallots

¼ cup harissa (see here)

Sea salt, to taste

¼ cup celery leaves

¼ cup pickled shallots (see here)

½ cup thinly sliced French breakfast radishes

1 Tbsp cold-pressed olive oil

6 nigella seed crackers (see here)

¼ cup dukkah spice (see here)

NIGELLA CRACKERS In a stand mixer fitted with a paddle attachment, combine dry ingredients and mix well. Gradually pour in water and oil and mix on medium speed for 3 minutes. Wrap dough in plastic wrap and chill for 1 hour.

Preheat oven to 350°F.

Place dough onto a large piece of parchment paper and roll to a thickness of ¼ inch. Put parchment paper onto a baking sheet and bake for 6 to 7 minutes. Rotate pan halfway and bake for another 6 to 7 minutes, until lightly golden brown.

Lightly brush with oil and gently sprinkle with sea salt. Using your hands, break into crackers of your desired serving size and shape.

LAMB TARTARE In a stainless steel mixing bowl, combine lamb, chopped radishes, chopped shallots, and harissa. Season with sea salt to taste.

In a separate bowl, combine celery leaves, pickled shallots, and breakfast radishes. Add oil and season with salt.

Plate a large scoop of the lamb tartare on a serving dish and arrange the salad to the side. Garnish with dukkah spice and sea salt. Serve with nigella crackers.

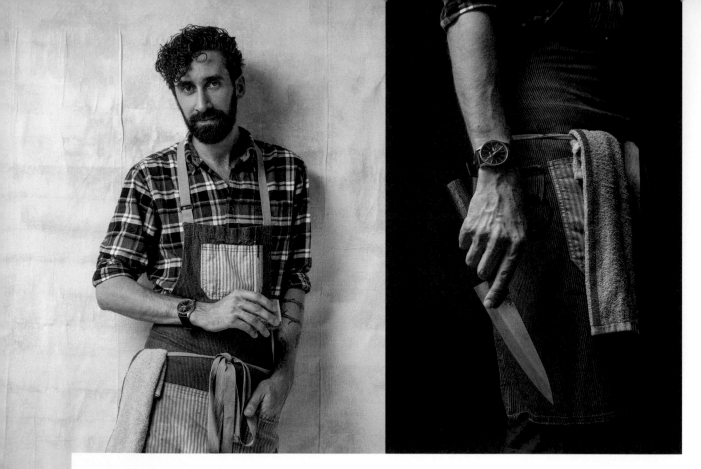

San Fermo Samuel West

HISTORY HAS been an important backdrop for Samuel West. San Fermo—the hyper-charming cottage-style trattoria he helped open (along with his father, a co-owner) in 2016—resuscitated the once-residential Pioneer Houses on Ballard Avenue. Sure, he spent time on the lines at Oddfellows, Staple & Fancy, and Anchovies & Olives, but most of his skills as an executive chef have been sharpened on the job, cooking for a packed house, night after night.

Talk about diving in feet first. What keeps him sane is his deference to Italian culture and cuisine (he even jokes that he was probably Italian in a past life). The plot to his first trip to Italy goes something like this: Teenager saves up enough money to travel to Italy to "find himself." He first settles near Venice in a monastery named San Fermo, then moves in with a family friend only to spend countless nights playing gin rummy, drinking bulk red wine, and cooking carbonara. Teenager moves back home to Seattle and eventually becomes the chef of an Italian family restaurant named after the monastery that changed his life. (Fade out and cue end credits.)

Speaking of the carbonara, it is made with fresh egg yolk, black pepper, guanciale, and Pecorino, and it also happens to be a staple on San Fermo's menu. And if it's not listed, you can order it anyway. However, the dish that's even closer to West's heart is the Spaghetti Bolognese. "My dad and I have been making the same recipes since I was a kid," says West. "It will always be on the menu."

→ Rabbit Cacciatore

BRINE

4 qts (16 cups) water

4 cups salt

1 cup granulated sugar

3 bay leaves

2 sprigs fresh thyme

1 Tbsp dried juniper berries

1 Tbsp red pepper flakes

RABBIT

2 red bell peppers

2 yellow bell peppers

4 qts (16 cups) brine (see here)

8 rabbit legs

5 Tbsp extra-virgin olive oil (divided)

3 cloves garlic, crushed

1½ cups dry white wine (divided)

2 to 3 qts (8 to 12 cups) chicken stock

4 cups canned crushed tomatoes

1 cup Castelvetrano olives, pitted

1 to 2 tsp freshly squeezed lemon juice

2 Tbsp chopped fresh thyme

1 bunch fresh parsley, chopped, plus extra for garnish

Salt, to taste

Polenta, to serve (see here)

Rabbit Cacciatore

SERVES 4

Brining helps to retain moisture and tenderize the meat. Chef Samuel West adds juniper berries, bay leaves, thyme, and red pepper flakes to the mixture, but feel free to use your preferred dried herbs and spices. The recipe can be made with chicken as well.

BRINE Combine ingredients in a large saucepan and bring to a boil over high heat. Reduce to medium heat and simmer for 5 minutes. Strain and chill in the fridge.

RABBIT Preheat oven to 400°F.

Place peppers on a baking sheet and roast for 40 minutes, turning them by a quarter every 10 minutes to ensure all sides are roasted, until surface is charred and peppers have collapsed slightly. (Alternatively, use a broiler to roast, but keep a close eye on the peppers to prevent them from burning.)

Place peppers in a bowl and cover with plastic wrap for 15 minutes. Slice each pepper from top to bottom and remove stem and seeds. Peel off the charred skin, then slice into ½-inch-thick strips.

Remove saucepan of brine from the fridge, add rabbit, and submerge completely. Refrigerate for 30 minutes, covering with parchment paper if you like, but it's not necessary. Remove rabbit from brine, rinse under cold running water, and pat dry with a clean dish towel. Set aside.

Heat 2 tablespoons oil in a large Dutch oven over medium-high heat. Add garlic and sauté for 10 to 15 seconds, until golden brown. Deglaze with the 1 cup wine, then add peppers, stock, tomatoes, and olives. Bring to a boil, then reduce heat to medium-low, and simmer for 30 minutes. Season to taste with salt and lemon juice.

Preheat oven to 250°F.

3 cups chicken stock
1 cup heavy cream
1 cup fine yellow cornmeal
¼ cup (½ stick) salted butter
Salt, to taste

In a large cast-iron skillet, heat remaining 3 tablespoons of olive oil over high heat until oil begins to ripple. Sear rabbit legs for 1 minute on each side, until golden brown. Discard oil and deglaze the pan with the remaining ½ cup wine. Using a wooden spoon or spatula, scrape the bits from the bottom of the pan and add to the braising sauce.

Add rabbit to sauce, cover, and braise for 3 hours. Stir in thyme and parsley and season to taste with salt. Keep warm until ready to serve.

POLENTA Bring stock and cream to a boil in a medium saucepan. Reduce to medium heat and add cornmeal. Using a wooden spoon or spatula, stir continuously and scrape the bottom to avoid any scorching. Cook until polenta has thickened and begins to spit. Reduce to low heat and cook for 45 minutes, stirring occasionally.

Add butter and whisk, removing any lumps. Season with salt.

PLATING Put polenta onto each plate, add two legs, and ladle braising sauce overtop. Garnish with parsley and serve.

ROSEMARY-INFUSED OLIVE OIL

1 cup olive oil

2 sprigs fresh rosemary

ROSEMARY FARINATA

1 cup chickpea flour

1 cup lukewarm water

½ cup rosemary-infused olive oil (see here)

1 tsp kosher salt

1 to 2 Tbsp extra-virgin olive oil

½ tsp chopped fresh rosemary

Coarse sea salt, for finishing

Rosemary Farinata

SERVES 2 TO 4

Farinata is an Italian chickpea pancake from the province of Liguria. At San Fermo, it's served with a soft house-made cheese (cagliata) and tomato confit, but the dish is substantial enough to be served on its own.

ROSEMARY-INFUSED OLIVE OIL Pour oil into a slow cooker set on low, add rosemary, and steep for 1 hour. (Alternatively, heat oil and rosemary in a saucepan over very low heat, but take care and watch that it doesn't burn.) Set aside.

ROSEMARY FARINATA Combine chickpea flour, water, rosemary-infused olive oil, and salt and whisk until smooth and the consistency of buttermilk. Cover with plastic wrap and let sit at room temperature overnight, or at least 2 hours. (The longer the better.)

Preheat oven to 450°F.

Heat 1 tablespoon extra-virgin olive oil in a 10-inch cast-iron skillet (enough to thinly cover the bottom) and warm in the oven for 5 minutes. Remove the pan from the oven and pour in the batter. Return to the oven and bake for 10 minutes, or until the pancake is firm and the edges set. Heat the broiler. (Lightly brush the top of the pancake with another table-spoon of olive oil if it looks dry.) Broil a few inches from the heat for 2 minutes, or until top starts to brown.

PLATING Cut pancake into wedges, and finish on individual plates with fresh rosemary and coarse salt. Serve hot or warm.

Scout Derek Simcik

SEATTLE IS a destination that offers countless opportunities for international travelers and culinary transplants to shine. One such newcomer is Derek Simcik. An alumnus of the Kimpton Hotel group, Simcik has opened hotel restaurants in Washington, D.C., Chicago, and, most recently, Santa Barbara, and his hospitality chops give the most senior industry vets a run for their money. Cool fact: his dad was a CIA agent, which not only makes for a fantastic ice breaker in any social situation, but provided Simcik the opportunity to see the world through the lens of other countries via constant travel. He put his nomadic lifestyle on hold when he moved to Seattle in 2016 to become the executive chef at the Thompson Hotel.

His experiences translate into an edible story, which Simcik applies to approachable and familiar dishes, either in the form of ingredient or technique.

The summer rockfish is a perfect example. Accompanied by fresh corn—some fermented, some used as a "pudding" base—it reflects the southern heritage of Simcik's parents. And while he gets excited about switching up the menu and pushing its boundaries, his priority is to play the role of the accommodating, gracious host to a never-ending dinner party. It's a familiar hat that he wears well.

→ Tomato Salad with Crispy Speck and Whipped Fromage Blanc

CHARRED TOMATO VINAIGRETTE

2 large heirloom tomatoes, halved

¼ cup red wine vinegar

1 tsp finely chopped garlic

2 Tbsp finely chopped shallots

2 Tbsp chopped fresh basil

½ tsp fennel seeds

½ tsp freshly ground black pepper

1 tsp granulated sugar

Salt, to taste

2 Tbsp sherry vinegar, plus more if needed

⅓ cup extra-virgin olive oil

CRISPY SPECK

5½ oz speck or prosciutto, cut into paper-thin slices

Olive oil, for drizzling

WHIPPED FROMAGE BLANC

2 cups fromage blanc

Zest of 1 lemon

Salt and freshly ground pepper, to taste

ASSEMBLY

5 to 6 heirloom tomatoes, cut into wedges

Charred tomato vinaigrette (see here)

Fresh basil leaves, torn, for garnish

Salt, to taste

Tomato Salad with Crispy Speck and Whipped Fromage Blanc

SERVES 4 TO 6

Chef Derek Simcik prepares this perfect summer starter with fromage blanc, a soft cheese made with whole milk. With less fat than cream cheese, it adds a delicate sour note. You can also substitute the fromage blanc with crème fraîche.

CHARRED TOMATO VINAIGRETTE Preheat grill to high heat. Grill tomatoes for 2 to 4 minutes, turning occasionally, until charred.

Combine tomatoes, red wine vinegar, garlic, shallot, basil, fennel seeds, pepper, sugar, and salt in a bowl. Blend with a stick blender and allow to macerate for at least 8 hours. Strain through a cheesecloth into a bowl.

For every 1 cup of charred tomato water (strained mixture), add 2 tablespoons sherry vinegar. Whisking continuously, gradually add oil and blend until emulsified. Adjust salt to taste, if needed, and set aside.

CRISPY SPECK Preheat oven to 275°F. Line a baking sheet with parchment paper.

Lay speck (or prosciutto) on the prepared baking sheet in a single layer (do not overlap). Lightly drizzle oil overtop and bake for 20 minutes, or until crispy. Remove and set aside to cool.

WHIPPED FROMAGE BLANC In a stand mixer fitted with a whisk attachment, whisk fromage blanc on medium speed for 2 to 3 minutes, or until medium peaks start to form. Add lemon zest and salt and pepper and whisk for another 2 minutes, until stiff peaks form.

Scoop whipped fromage blanc into a piping bag and refrigerate until needed.

ASSEMBLY Combine tomatoes and vinaigrette in a bowl and toss.

Scoop a few large spoonfuls of tomatoes into individual bowls, then pipe dollops of whipped fromage blanc on top. Garnish with crispy speck (or prosciutto), broken into shards, and basil. Season with salt and serve.

CORN CREAM

4 cups heavy cream

6 ears corn, kernels cut off (about 6 cups), both kernels and ears reserved

2 bay leaves

1 Tbsp whole black peppercorns

CORN SUCCOTASH

1 Tbsp vegetable oil

2 Tbsp finely chopped shallots

2 Tbsp finely chopped garlic

½ cup chopped red bell pepper

½ cup chopped yellow bell pepper

6 cups reserved corn kernels

2 cups cooked yellow eye beans or cannellini beans (if canned, drained and rinsed)

½ cup white wine

¼ cup corn cream (see here)

¼ cup (½ stick) unsalted butter

Salt, to taste

Rockfish with Corn Succotash, Brown Butter Corn Crumble, and Corn Beurre Blanc

SERVES 4

Inspired by chef Derek Simcik's southern roots, this dish has all the makings of a refined comfort food: it's got the play on corn chowder, a bit of succotash, and a delicious crumble. And with its striking presentation, this is a standout dish to serve guests.

CORN CREAM Combine cream, corn ears, bay leaves, and peppercorns in a heavy-bottomed saucepan over medium-low heat. Simmer for 15 minutes. Remove from heat and set aside to steep for another 30 minutes.

Strain mixture through a fine-mesh strainer and cool to room temperature. Set aside.

CORN SUCCOTASH Heat oil in a heavy-bottomed skillet over medium-high heat. Add shallots and garlic and sauté for 2 minutes, until fragrant but not browned (reduce heat if necessary). Add peppers and sauté for another 2 to 3 minutes, until softened.

Stir in corn and beans and sauté for 3 to 5 minutes. Pour in wine and reduce, until most of it has evaporated. Add corn cream, reduce heat to medium-low, and cook for another 3 to 5 minutes, until reduced by a little more than half.

Stir in butter until fully incorporated and thickened. Season to taste with salt.

CONTINUED OVERLEAF

BROWN BUTTER CORN CRUMBLE

Cooking spray

¾ cup (1½ sticks) unsalted butter (divided)

2 eggs

1½ cups buttermilk

1½ cups water

1 cup cornmeal

1 cup all-purpose flour

⅔ cup granulated sugar

½ tsp baking soda

½ tsp salt

CORN BEURRE BLANC

¼ cup dry white wine

¼ cup white wine vinegar

2 Tbsp finely chopped shallots

⅓ cup corn cream (see here)

¼ tsp salt, plus extra to taste

1 cup (2 sticks) cold unsalted butter, cut into 1-inch cubes

Freshly ground black pepper, to taste

BROWN BUTTER CORN CRUMBLE Preheat oven to 375°F. Line a baking sheet with parchment paper and spray with cooking spray.

Put ½ cup (1 stick) butter into a bowl and melt in the microwave. Set aside to cool to room temperature. Combine melted butter, eggs, buttermilk, and water in a bowl and mix well.

In a separate bowl, combine cornmeal, flour, sugar, baking soda, and salt and mix well. Pour wet mixture into dry and mix well until fully incorporated.

Pour batter into a 9-inch baking pan and cover with foil. Bake for 30 to 40 minutes, until a skewer inserted into the bread's center comes out clean. Set aside to cool. Reduce oven temperature to 250°F.

Break up corn bread, put into a food processor, and pulse until crumbled.

In a large sauté pan, melt ¼ cup (½ stick) butter over medium heat, until the butter solids are lightly brown. Add crumbled corn bread and stir until well mixed. Spread the crumble onto the prepared baking sheet and bake for 20 to 30 minutes, until dry. Set aside.

CORN BEURRE BLANC Combine wine, vinegar, and shallots in a large heavy-bottomed saucepan over medium heat and boil for 5 minutes, or until syrupy and reduced to 3 tablespoons. Add corn cream and salt and boil for 1 minute.

Reduce heat to medium-low and add 2 to 3 tablespoons butter, whisking constantly until liquefied. Repeat in small batches, lifting pan from the heat occasionally (before it starts to bubble), until all butter is used and the sauce is a smooth, firm consistency like hollandaise.

ROCKFISH

4 (5-oz) skin-on
    rockfish fillets
Salt, to taste
2 Tbsp vegetable oil
2 Tbsp unsalted butter

Remove from heat, season to taste with salt and pepper, and strain sauce through a medium-mesh strainer. Discard shallots.

ROCKFISH Preheat oven to 400°F. Pat fillets dry with a paper towel and season both sides with salt.

Heat a heavy-bottomed ovenproof French steel pan or nonstick skillet over medium heat. Add oil and just before it begins to smoke, lay fillets skin side down in the pan, carefully pressing down with fingers to prevent the rockfish from curling up. Cook for 2 to 3 minutes until the skin is golden brown.

Put pan into the oven and cook for 8 minutes, until fish is nearly cooked through. Return pan to the stove top and use a fish spatula to carefully flip the fillets. Add butter and use a spoon to baste melted butter over them.

Transfer fillets to a plate lined with paper towels to drain.

PLATING Place a few generous spoonfuls of succotash in center of four plates and top each with a fillet. Spoon corn beurre blanc around the rockfish and succotash and top with a few spoonfuls of corn crumble. Serve immediately.

Single Shot Brad Kelleher

BRAD KELLEHER, a scrappy kid from Bear Creek, was raised in the restaurant industry. His mom was a server for the better part of his childhood, and kitchens were often his babysitter. When he realized he wanted to make cooking his career, he talked his way into a job at Tilth, where he moved up from pantry chef to sous chef in four years. In 2015, Kelleher landed at Single Shot, the polished neighborhood restaurant on the west slope of Capitol Hill named after the giant antique shotgun that hangs above the cocktail bar.

Within the walls of this comfortable 40-seat nook, Kelleher bangs out unexpectedly refined dishes from a super snug kitchen. Willie's Farm baby lettuce is artfully served with Black Mission figs, marcona almonds, and ricotta salata. Pacific halibut is baked with marjoram *beurre monté* (butter sauce), wood sorrel, and sea beans. (He even fries the fish skin to make a nori-dusted chicharron.) Rum, cherry, and toasted coconut make the perfect complement to wild chamomile ice cream.

These thoughtful touches make Kelleher's food both delicious and visually stunning, which is a fitting irony considering the location of Single Shot was a photography studio in a former life. There's a quiet confidence to Kelleher's understated menu, proving that big ideas often come from humble beginnings.

SAUCE GRIBICHE

6 eggs

¼ cup capers, chopped

¼ cup caper brine

¼ cup chopped fresh Italian parsley

¼ cup finely chopped fresh chives

1 Tbsp Dijon mustard

1 cup extra-virgin olive oil

3 Tbsp freshly squeezed lemon juice

Salt and freshly ground black pepper

ASPARAGUS

2 bunches asparagus, trimmed

Salt, to taste

Microgreens, for garnish

Juice of ½ lemon (optional)

Extra-virgin olive oil, for drizzling (optional)

Blanched Asparagus with Sauce Gribiche

SERVES 6 TO 8

Mid-spring to early summer is the best time to get asparagus in Washington. Make sure to either peel the ends to remove the tough outer skins, or trim the ends altogether before cooking.

SAUCE GRIBICHE Put whole eggs into a heavy-bottomed saucepan and add enough cold water to cover. Place on high heat for 20 to 25 minutes. Transfer eggs to a bowl of ice water to cool, then peel. Finely chop and put them into a large bowl. (At the restaurant, the eggs are pressed through a wire rack to create the perfect dice. For a more rustic look, use a stiff wire whisk to smash the eggs in the bottom of the bowl until you reach the desired size.)

Add capers, caper brine, parsley, chives, and mustard and mix. Pour in oil and lemon juice and mix well using a rubber spatula. Season with salt and pepper to taste and set aside.

ASPARAGUS Fill a stockpot halfway with water and bring to a boil. Gently lower asparagus into pot and blanch for 5 minutes. Using a slotted spoon, transfer asparagus to a bowl of ice water. Drain.

Place asparagus spears in a clean bowl and season with salt. Using your hands, mix it into the asparagus.

Arrange asparagus on a large serving platter and top with dollops of gribiche. Garnish with microgreens. Season with a drizzle of olive oil and a squeeze of lemon, if using. Salt to taste, if desired.

LEMON CURD

½ cup granulated sugar

½ cup freshly squeezed lemon juice

⅓ cup (⅔ stick) unsalted butter

3 eggs

PANCAKE BATTER

1 cup all-purpose flour, plus extra if needed

2 Tbsp granulated sugar

1 tsp baking powder

½ tsp salt

1 cup buttermilk

¾ cup whole milk

2 Tbsp unsalted butter, melted

1 egg

ASSEMBLY

1 Tbsp unsalted butter

1 recipe pancake batter (see here)

¼ cup huckleberries

¼ cup crumbled chèvre (we prefer Laura Chenel's)

Confectioners' sugar, for dusting

Maple syrup, for drizzling

Fresh mint leaves, torn, for garnish (optional)

Huckleberry Pancakes with Lemon Curd and Chèvre

SERVES 2

"My goal with this recipe was to come up with the city's second-best pancake—aiming for the best pancake is too much pressure," says chef Kelleher. "But most of our customers will vouch for this being the ultimate pancake in Seattle."

LEMON CURD Combine ingredients in a small saucepan and whisk over medium-low heat, until the whisk leaves marks in the curd. Remove from heat and transfer to a bowl. Chill in the fridge for 30 to 45 minutes, or until mixture is thick but not stiff.

PANCAKE BATTER In a large bowl, combine flour, sugar, baking powder, and salt and mix well. In a separate bowl, combine buttermilk, milk, butter, and egg and whisk until well mixed.

Slowly pour wet ingredients into dry ingredients. Use a rubber spatula to fold ingredients together, until mixed but still lumpy. (If your batter is too crepe-like, add more flour.) Cover and set aside at room temperature for 5 minutes.

ASSEMBLY Melt butter in an 8-inch nonstick skillet over medium-high heat. Pour in ¼ cup of batter and tilt pan to spread it out evenly. Add berries and cook for 3 minutes, or until golden. Flip and cook for another 2 minutes, or until golden brown. Remove from heat. Repeat with remaining pancakes. (Any unused batter can be stored in the fridge for up to a week.)

PLATING Place a serving of pancakes on plate. Top with 2 tablespoons of curd and 2 tablespoons of chèvre. Dust with confectioners' sugar, drizzle with maple syrup, garnish with mint, if using, and serve immediately.

Stoneburner Jason Stoneburner

WHEN JASON STONEBURNER talks about his cooking philosophy, it's difficult to discern whether he's talking about food or his second love: surfing. Words like "fun," "interesting," and "not too serious" are used aplenty and his dishes are a reflection of his inviting and casual attitude.

His favorite pastime has led him around the world, and the dishes at his eponymous restaurant in the boutique Hotel Ballard reflect his experiences. And Seattle is all the better for it. What started out as a mostly Mediterranean-leaning menu now borrows from international flavors, with Stoneburner often searching out parallels between cuisines and melding ingredients that make sense naturally. For instance, spaghettini, udon, and ramen noodles all have similar textures and preparation, which explains why the unusual—yet utterly delicious—togarashi spaghettini

with Dungeness crab, scallion, and ginger might feature on his menu.

Other dishes like cauliflower served with salsa negra and pickled onions and octopus with patatas, mojo verde, and fresno draw inspiration from Mexico, which is practically a second home for the chef.

Interesting? Check. Fun? Check. Not too serious? Check. To Stoneburner, who also oversees the French-inspired Bastille across the street, cooking, like surfing, is about balance and having a good time.

→ Capunti with Calabrian
Sausage Ragu

CAPUNTI

1½ cups water, room temperature

Pinch of saffron

2 cups durum flour

2 cups semolina flour

CALABRIAN SAUSAGE RAGU

1 lb ground pork

1 Tbsp sweet smoked paprika

2 tsp Calabrian chili powder

1½ tsp sea salt, plus extra to taste

1 tsp fennel seeds

1 Tbsp olive oil

½ cup plus 2 Tbsp white wine

1 cup chicken stock

1 bay leaf

¾ cup plus 2 Tbsp tomato purée or tomato sauce

¾ cup tomato juice

Capunti with Calabrian Sausage Ragu

SERVES 4 TO 6

Capunti is a short, oval pasta that resembles an open pea pod. Chef Jason Stoneburner usually serves these toothsome noodles with hearty meat sauces and recommends using ground pork butt—just ask your butcher to grind it for you. The pasta is complemented by vegetables just as well.

CAPUNTI Combine water and saffron in a bowl and set aside to steep for at least 15 minutes.

In a large bowl, combine flours, mix well, and create a well in the center. Strain the saffron water into the well and use a fork to mix flour into water until the mixture becomes shaggy.

On a clean work surface dusted with flour, knead dough until it is smooth and elastic. Roll dough into a ball, then store it in a plastic bag at room temperature for 20 minutes to rest.

Working in batches, roll a piece of dough into a ½- × 18-inch rope. Slice into 2-inch lengths. Using your index, middle, and ring fingers, press down into dough to flatten slightly, then roll 180 degrees to create a curved shape. Repeat until all the pasta has been formed. The capunti can be placed on a tray and frozen or set aside until use.

CALABRIAN SAUSAGE RAGU In a large bowl, combine pork, paprika, chili powder, salt, and fennel seeds and mix well.

Heat oil in a heavy-bottomed saucepan over medium-high heat, add sausage, and brown for 10 to 15 minutes, taking care not to break up sausage too fine.

Pour in wine and, using a wooden spoon, scrape the bits from the bottom of the pan. Reduce heat to medium-low and simmer for 5 minutes, until most of wine has evaporated. Add stock and bay leaf and simmer for another 20 minutes, until mixture has reduced by half.

Add tomato purée (or sauce) and tomato juice and simmer for 8 to 10 minutes, until thickened. Discard bay leaf.

ASSEMBLY
3 Tbsp unsalted butter
Pinch of fresh marjoram
  leaves, plus extra for
  garnish
Salt, to taste
Grated Pecorino Romano or
  Parmesan, to serve

ASSEMBLY Bring a large saucepan of salted water to a boil. Add pasta and cook for 5 to 8 minutes, until they rise to the surface. (Always nab one from the water to check for doneness.) Drain.

Add butter and marjoram leaves to the ragu, then adjust the seasoning to taste with salt. Add drained pasta to the ragu pan and simmer for 2 to 3 minutes.

Garnish with marjoram and serve with grated Pecorino Romano (or Parmesan).

SALSA NEGRA

1½ cups grapeseed oil

10 guajillo chiles, stemmed and seeded (about 2 cups)

15 chiles de arbol, stemmed and seeded (about ½ cup)

½ cup chopped garlic

⅓ cup black garlic, peeled

¼ cup coconut sugar or brown sugar

2 Tbsp white wine vinegar

2 tsp cumin seeds

Sea salt, to taste

LIME-PICKLED ONIONS

1 red onion, top and bottom trimmed

2 cups freshly squeezed lime juice

½ tsp salt

ROASTED CAULIFLOWER

1 large head cauliflower

¼ cup grapeseed or olive oil

Salt and freshly ground black pepper, to taste

¼ cup chopped fresh cilantro, to serve

½ cup chopped fresh dill, to serve

Roasted Cauliflower with Lime-Pickled Onions and Salsa Negra

SERVES 2 TO 4

Cauliflower has a steak-like quality when cut into large wedges. The charred surface makes a nice contrast to a slightly crunchy interior. Just be sure to make extra salsa negra—you'll want to spoon it over everything.

SALSA NEGRA Heat oil in a skillet over medium heat, add chiles, and roast for 5 minutes, or until skins are brown and fragrant. Transfer to a plate and set aside.

Add remaining ingredients to the skillet and cook over medium heat for 3 to 5 minutes. Set aside to cool.

Transfer mixture and the roasted chiles to a blender and blend until smooth. Season to taste with salt. (Makes 2 cups)

LIME-PICKLED ONIONS Cut the onion in half through the root. Using a mandoline, thinly slice each onion along the grain. Rinse under cold running water (to mellow out the heat) and drain.

Put onion slices into a bowl, pour lime juice in, making sure the onion is covered, and add salt. Set aside for 1 hour, then drain. (Makes about 2 cups)

ROASTED CAULIFLOWER Preheat grill to medium-high heat.

Place the cauliflower on its crown and quarter into 4 large equal pieces through the top of the stem. (The edible core will hold the cauliflower together during grilling.) Transfer the pieces to a large bowl and drizzle with oil, season with salt and pepper, and toss.

Put cauliflower on the grill and grill each side for 3 to 5 minutes, until charred all over.

PLATING Transfer to a serving platter and spoon salsa negra overtop. Top with lime-pickled onions and then garnish with cilantro and dill. Serve.

Surrell Aaron Tekulve

HAVING GROWN up in small-town Coram, Montana, Aaron Tekulve is still blown away by the abundance of fresh produce in the Pacific Northwest. He moved to Seattle to pursue music (he was the drummer in a rock band called Your Divine Tragedy), but it was ultimately a culinary career that won him over. "I love this place because it has real seasons," he says, "and we still have things to cook in the winter—unlike Montana, where all ingredients come from California or the freezer."

While studying culinary arts at the Art Institute of Seattle, Tekulve started working under John Sundstrom at the esteemed Lark and learned the art of creating beautiful, rustic food and building large flavors with a subtle hand.

Much like a composer, Tekulve can visualize the food in his head before he creates it: "I orchestrate menus in my head, imagining how dishes will look and taste. I could never do this with music as a drummer, which is why I find greater satisfaction with cooking."

Tekulve now focuses his attention on Surrell, his dinner series named after his mom and grandmother (both have it as a middle name), whom he credits for nurturing his curiosity toward food. At Surrell, Tekulve creates four- to eight-course menus that express the seasonality of the Pacific Northwest, and many of the ingredients are sourced within 30 miles of Seattle. A fall menu, for instance, might showcase ember-roasted baby rainbow carrots, root beer and sherry–braised beef cheeks, and burnt pumpkin panna cotta with dark chocolate. "As a chef, creativity is huge for me," he says. "Then to share that with friends, family, or complete strangers? Those are the big wins."

→ Burnt Wood Ice Cream with Chocolate Ganache and Red Wine Huckleberries

PICKLED SEA BEANS

¼ cup sea beans (you can substitute fresh French green beans, cut into 1-inch lengths)

1 cup white wine vinegar

1 bay leaf

1 tsp granulated sugar

1 tsp whole black peppercorns

½ tsp salt

HERB SAUCE

¼ cup (½ stick) unsalted butter

¼ cup coarsely chopped shallots

1 Tbsp coarsely chopped garlic

2 to 3 Tbsp salt, plus extra to taste

4 cups spinach

¼ cup fresh tarragon leaves

¼ cup fresh dill fronds

¼ cup fresh basil leaves

Pinch of xanthan gum (optional)

Sockeye Salmon Confit with Shaved Fennel, Pickled Sea Beans, and Charred Turnips

SERVES 4

Living in the Pacific Northwest and eating salmon are synonymous. While there may be a dozen ways to prepare salmon, chef Aaron Tekulve's version will have you cooking it to perfection. Sea beans are plentiful at summer farmers' markets and are stocked by many Asian grocers.

PICKLED SEA BEANS Place sea beans in a glass or plastic bowl.

In a small saucepan, combine vinegar, bay leaf, sugar, peppercorns, and salt and bring to a boil over high heat. Remove from heat and set aside to cool down to room temperature.

Strain mixture into the bowl of sea beans, making sure beans are completely covered. Refrigerate until needed.

HERB SAUCE Melt butter in a small saucepan over medium heat, add shallots and garlic and sauté for 2 to 3 minutes until softened but not caramelized. Remove from heat and transfer mixture to a high-power blender (such as a Vitamix).

Add the salt to a saucepan of water and bring to a boil. Add spinach, tarragon, dill, and basil and cook for 5 to 10 seconds until wilted and bright green. Drain spinach and herbs and rinse under cold running water, until cooled. Transfer spinach, herbs, and xanthan gum, if using, to the blender and blend on low. Increase speed and add cold water, if necessary, to loosen mixture. Increase to high speed and blend for 2 to 3 minutes, or until very smooth.

Pour herb sauce into an airtight container and refrigerate immediately, until needed.

SALMON

2 sprigs fresh thyme

1 bunch fresh dill

1 bunch fresh tarragon

2 bay leaves

4 large garlic cloves, sliced

Peel of 2 lemons

4 (6-oz) portions skinless sockeye salmon, pinbones removed

Salt and freshly ground black pepper, to taste

2 qts (8 cups) grapeseed oil

2 turnips (baby or regular) peeled and cut into 8 to 10 wedges

2 large bulbs fennel

¼ cup pickled sea beans (see here)

2 Tbsp finely chopped preserved lemons

2 Tbsp finely chopped fresh Italian parsley

3 Tbsp high-quality extra-virgin olive oil (such as Arbequina), plus extra for drizzling

2 Tbsp freshly squeezed lemon juice

Fleur de sel, to taste

SALMON In a large roasting pan, evenly spread out thyme, dill, tarragon, bay leaves, garlic slices, and lemon peels.

Season salmon with salt and pepper and place on top of herbs in pan, spacing them at least ½ inch apart. Set aside for 15 to 20 minutes to allow the fish to absorb the salt.

Pour enough grapeseed oil into the pan to fully cover salmon. Heat pan over medium-low heat, until temperature reaches 145°F. Cook fish for 15 to 20 minutes for medium, or until it's light pinkish orange and slightly firm. (Be sure to maintain temperature throughout the cooking process.)

Carefully remove salmon from the oil and reserve at room temperature or refrigerate until ready to serve. (This can be done up to a day or two in advance.)

Meanwhile, heat a cast-iron skillet over high heat. Add turnips cut side down to a dry skillet in a single layer and cook for 2 to 3 minutes, until charred. Flip turnips and char on the other side for another 2 to 3 minutes until fully charred and tender. Remove from heat and set aside.

ASSEMBLY Using a mandoline, shave fennel very thinly and place into a medium bowl. (Discard the cores.) Add sea beans, preserved lemon, turnips, parsley, and olive oil and mix well. Season with 1 to 2 tablespoons lemon juice and salt to taste.

PLATING Spoon herb sauce onto the plate. Place a piece of salmon on the plate, season with a few drops of lemon juice and a sprinkle of fleur de sel. Place a large spoonful of fennel salad next to the salmon and drizzle with olive oil. Serve.

CHOCOLATE GANACHE

6 oz dark chocolate,
   70% cacao (we prefer
   Theo's chocolate),
   coarsely chopped

¾ cup heavy cream

3 Tbsp corn syrup

1 Tbsp smoked sea salt

1 Tbsp finely chopped
   cocoa nibs

RED WINE HUCKLEBERRIES

2 cups huckleberries
   (divided)

1 cup red wine, such as
   Cabernet Sauvignon

½ cup granulated sugar

1 star anise

Pinch of freshly ground
   black pepper

Burnt Wood Ice Cream with Chocolate Ganache and Red Wine Huckleberries

SERVES 4

There's no better place to ignite the memory of campfires like the great outdoors of the Pacific Northwest. Chef Tekulve has figured out a way to enhance his food with that very same smoky euphoria: "Growing up in Montana at the base of Glacier National Park, I have incredible memories of cooking over a campfire and using that delicious smoke to season our food."

CHOCOLATE GANACHE Line bottom of four (3-inch) ring molds with foil and place on a baking sheet.

Put chocolate into a medium heatproof bowl.

In a small saucepan, combine cream and corn syrup and bring to a simmer over medium heat. Turn off the heat and place the bowl of chocolate on top of the pot, stirring for 2 to 3 minutes, until chocolate begins to melt. Pour hot cream over chocolate and whisk until glossy and chocolate has melted completely.

Pour the chocolate mixture evenly into the ring molds, gently tapping them to flatten the surface. Garnish with smoked sea salt and chopped cocoa nibs. Refrigerate for at least 2 hours.

To release chocolate ganaches from the ring molds, remove foil from bottom and wrap your hands around the molds to gently warm. Gently release them from the molds. Place on parchment paper or in an airtight container until needed.

RED WINE HUCKLEBERRIES In a small saucepan, combine 1 cup huckleberries, red wine, sugar, star anise, and pepper. Bring to a simmer over medium heat and cook for 10 to 15 minutes, stirring occasionally, until thick like maple syrup.

Transfer mixture to a blender and purée until smooth. Strain through a fine-mesh strainer.

Place remaining cup of huckleberries in a small bowl, add red wine mixture, and set aside.

BURNT WOOD ICE CREAM

2 cups uncured
  hickory chips
3 cups whole milk
3 cups heavy cream
2 vanilla beans, split
  lengthwise and scraped
1 tsp vanilla extract
12 egg yolks
1½ cups granulated sugar

1 Tbsp smoked sea salt
½ cup dehydrated nonfat
  milk powder
Micro basil leaves,
  for garnish

Note: For a smokier flavor, place the cream and egg mixture (crème anglaise) and hickory chips in a smoker and smoke for 10 minutes. Stir mixture and taste for smokiness. Repeat as desired. Alternatively, use a PolyScience smoking gun: tightly wrap the bowl of crème anglaise with plastic wrap and pierce a small hole into the top of the plastic. Insert hose into hole and smoke, until bowl is smoky. Remove hose, cover hole with a small piece of plastic wrap, and set aside for 15 to 20 minutes. Repeat as necessary to achieve the desired smokiness. Continue to make ice cream according to manufacturer's instructions.

BURNT WOOD ICE CREAM Add hickory chips to a large pot. Using a kitchen torch, burn the chips, until three-quarters are charred. Pour in milk and cream, stir, and set on very low heat for 1 hour. Strain into a large bowl, using a fine-mesh strainer. Measure 4 cups of the hickory cream and pour it into a clean saucepan. Add vanilla seeds and extract and bring to a simmer over medium heat. Remove from heat.

Meanwhile, place a metal bowl in a large bowl filled with ice. Set aside.

In a medium bowl, combine egg yolks, sugar, smoked sea salt, and milk powder and mix well. Add 2 to 3 tablespoons of hickory cream to the bowl and whisk continuously. Repeat until half of cream mixture is used. Add egg mixture to saucepan of hickory cream and cook over medium-low heat. Using a silicone spatula, slowly and continuously stir mixture until it reaches a temperature of 175°F. Remove from heat.

Strain mixture into the bowl set over the prepared ice bath, then refrigerate for 30 to 45 minutes, until cooled. Pour cooled mixture into an ice-cream maker and freeze according to the manufacturer's instructions. (Makes 1½ quarts)

PLATING Place a disc of the dark chocolate ganache on each plate. Drizzle 2 to 3 large spoonfuls of the red wine huckleberries around the plate and on the ganache. Place a scoop or quenelle of ice cream on top of each ganache disc and garnish with micro basil leaves.

Sushi Kappo Tamura Taichi Kitamura

SUSHI KAPPO TAMURA (SKT) is a Seattle institution, and chef-co-owner Taichi Kitamura is a big reason for that. As soon as you enter this sleek Eastlake kappo-style restaurant, Kitamura is front and center, greeting those approaching the 13-seat sushi bar with his signature cherubic smile. Service here is just as important as the food, which is why the charismatic chef is behind the counter most nights. He loves meeting new people and preparing quality Japanese dishes with the wonderful bounty of the Pacific Northwest.

His hospitality is something he learned working at Shiro's under sushi master Shiro Kashiba, who has a knack for making customers happy. Kitamura recalls Shiro-san cracking the same jokes every night, and regardless of how repetitive or how obvious the geoduck metaphors became, diners were always engaged. And not only that, they were introduced to Japanese food culture in a fun way. It was a defining moment in Kitamura's life and a lesson he brought with him to SKT, where his charm is on par with his impeccable cuisine.

Each day, he finds out what ingredients are available, decides how to best prepare them, and then writes his menu. Seafood is often salted and grilled or served nigiri-style. He's introduced diners to new local foods such as the rich and buttery idiot fish (a bycatch of black cod) and the impossibly-hard-to-find Washington halibut. From spring to early fall, people go nuts for Kitamura's flash-steamed spot prawns with sake butter sauce. The rest of the year is no different: SKT has become the assignation of even the most discerning of sushi devotees, who are consistently wowed by one of the most skilled chefs in town.

1 (8-inch) piece kombu
  (see Note)

6 cups water

1 cup bonito flakes
  (see Note)

2 cups diced kabocha
  squash, cut into ½-inch
  pieces

½ small sweet onion,
  thinly sliced

3 to 4 Tbsp white miso

1 cup baby spinach

Note: Kombu (dried kelp) and dried bonito flakes can be found at Asian supermarkets.

Kabocha, Sweet Onion, and Spinach Miso Soup

SERVES 4
AS AN APPETIZER

Gently wipe kombu with a wet cloth and put into a large saucepan. Add water and soak for 1 hour. Bring to a boil over medium heat, removing the kombu just before boiling. Add bonito flakes, bring water to a full boil, and boil for 5 minutes. Remove from heat and set aside, until flakes settle to the bottom.

Strain this stock through cheesecloth or a fine-mesh strainer. Return stock to saucepan, add kabocha and onion, and bring to a boil. Reduce heat to medium and simmer for 3 minutes, until the kabocha is tender. Whisk in miso and add spinach. Ladle soup into bowls. Serve immediately.

2 cups short-grain rice

¼ cup rice vinegar

2 Tbsp cane sugar

1½ tsp sea salt

5 Tbsp soy sauce

1 Tbsp wasabi, plus extra
   to serve

4 oz sashimi-grade ahi tuna,
   cut into ½-inch cubes

4 oz sashimi-grade
   yellowtail (hamachi), cut
   into ½-inch cubes

4 oz sashimi-grade salmon,
   cut into ½-inch cubes

¼ cup finely chopped
   pickled sushi ginger

2 sheets nori seaweed,
   shredded into
   matchstick-sized strips

4 oz cooked bay shrimp

¼ cup salted salmon
   roe (ikura)

1 cup chopped English
   or Persian cucumber,
   unpeeled, cut in
   ½-inch cubes

Bara Chirashi

SERVES 4

Cook rice in a rice cooker according to manufacturer's instructions.
(If you don't have a rice cooker, you can cook rice on the stove top.)

Meanwhile, combine vinegar, sugar, and salt in a small saucepan and
heat over medium heat, until sugar and salt dissolve.

Transfer cooked rice to a large mixing bowl, add vinegar mixture, and
stir gently, without mashing the rice. Set aside to cool.

In a medium bowl, combine soy sauce and wasabi and mix well.
Add tuna, yellowtail, and salmon and mix well.

PLATING Put rice into a large shallow serving bowl. Top with ginger and
seaweed. Arrange fish, shrimp, salmon roe, and cucumbers on top. Serve
immediately, family-style, with additional wasabi, if desired.

Tavolàta Ethan Stowell

RESTAURATEUR ETHAN Stowell is a born host. You may think that's a no-brainer, but he had to open two very different restaurants to realize that he is happiest as a chef when his food takes a backseat to the experience of dining out. He provides a platform for a great evening and elevates a good time to a great time with simple Italian food.

Tavolàta opened in 2007, five years after Stowell's first restaurant, Union. And while Union was a restaurant where Stowell could show off his chef skills, he changed his tune when he saw how much more fun customers were having at the less fussy Tavolàta—big groups were packing the communal table, hanging out, laughing, drinking, and feasting on boards of smoked trout bruschetta and huge bowls of rigatoni with spicy sausage. That's when the switch flipped. Stowell closed Union and began modeling his

progeny after Tavolàta, where a successful night is as dependent upon what the guests bring to the table as it is the great food.

Now, with more than a dozen restaurants in his camp, Stowell is rarely in the kitchen. Instead, he's hosting community and charity events, which have become the cornerstone of his business. In fact, he continues to open new restaurants so he can foster the multitude of causes he believes in. His philosophy: take care of your community and they'll take care of you.

FRIED BREAD CRUMBS

2 cloves garlic, crushed

¼ cup olive oil

½ baguette, stale or lightly toasted, sliced

Kosher salt

PASTA

1 lb bigoli pasta or spaghetti

¾ cup olive oil

3 cloves garlic, sliced

2 tsp red pepper flakes

12 oil-packed anchovy fillets, drained and chopped

¼ cup packed chopped fresh Italian parsley

¼ cup fried bread crumbs (see here)

Bigoli with Garlic, Chile, and Anchovy

SERVES 4

"This dish is Tavolàta's twist on *bigoli in salsa*, a traditional Venetian pasta that my wife, Angela, and I enjoyed in Italy," says Stowell. "If you can't find bigoli, use the best quality dried spaghetti you can find."

FRIED BREAD CRUMBS Heat garlic and oil in a saucepan over low heat and allow oil to infuse for 10 minutes.

Meanwhile, put baguette slices into a food processor and pulse to chop. Continue to process for 1 to 2 minutes, until finely ground. Add bread crumbs to garlic oil and cook over low heat for 2 to 3 minutes, until crumbs are toasted and have absorbed the oil. Season with salt. (Bread crumbs can be refrigerated in an airtight container for up to two weeks.)

PASTA Bring a large pot of salted water to a boil. Add pasta and cook for 1 minute less than directions on the package.

Meanwhile, heat oil in a large skillet over medium-low heat. Add garlic, red pepper flakes, and anchovies and cook for 30 seconds, stirring occasionally, until garlic has softened and anchovies have disintegrated.

Drain pasta, then tip into the skillet. Add parsley and toss well. Divide the pasta between four bowls and top each with a spoonful of bread crumbs. Serve immediately.

Canola oil, for frying

12 to 16 slices prosciutto

12 oz sushi-grade yellowtail (hamachi)

Salt, to taste

Juice of 1 lemon

¼ cup extra-virgin olive oil

4 tsp Taggiasca olives or any other oil-cured black olives, halved

16 to 20 small balls of cantaloupe (see Note)

Edible flowers, for garnish (optional)

Note: If you do not have a small melon baller for making cantaloupe balls, you can use a knife to cube them instead.

Hamachi Crudo with Fried Prosciutto, Taggiasca Olives, and Melon

SERVES 4

If you can't find hamachi, it's fine to use best-quality albacore tuna, ahi tuna, or fresh sea scallops in this dish.

Pour canola oil into a small saucepan to a depth of 2 inches and heat over medium-high heat to a temperature of 350°F. Fry prosciutto in batches (to prevent overcrowding) for 1 to 2 minutes, until crispy. Using a slotted spoon, transfer to a plate lined with paper towels. Set aside.

PLATING Slice the hamachi ¼ inch thick and divide among four dinner plates. Season with salt and lemon juice and drizzle with olive oil. Put olives, melon, and prosciutto onto each plate. Garnish with edible flowers, if using. Serve immediately.

Terra Plata Tamara Murphy

TAMARA MURPHY has slapped her name on some of Seattle's best food, starting at Dominique's Place, one of the city's premier French restaurants in the eighties. She led the kitchen for nearly a decade at Cafe Campagne and helped launch the careers of countless local chefs. As a chef who's never been interested in reinventing the wheel, Murphy's brilliance comes in the form of her pure passion for cooking. Beautiful produce and visits to local farmers keep her constantly inspired. "I try to buy from people who have a story," she says.

Each day at Terra Plata, Murphy showcases the authenticity of artisan products, along with the vegetables and herbs grown in the restaurant's rooftop garden. And after all these years, she's not interested in messing with what works. Her signature dish—the pork, clams, and chorizo—is a staple on all her menus.

The clams come from Taylor Shellfish, and she makes her own chorizo using local hogs.

Terra Plata is a beast of its own (much busier than her former restaurant, Brasa, ever was), yet Murphy continues to roll out good, consistent, warming food. We're talking savory Grilled Spot Prawns with roasted chiles and spices and an immensely satisfying Black Pepper Pappardelle with braised rabbit, chanterelles, peperonata, and pine nuts.

Her commitment to consistent, reliably delicious food has grounded Terra Plata as one of Capitol Hill's premier neighborhood restaurants. And even if the industry gets under her skin occasionally, Murphy never stops loving the act of feeding people.

BAGNA CAUDA

16 anchovy fillets
8 cloves garlic
1 cup olive oil
¼ cup heavy cream
2 Tbsp unsalted butter
Salt
Pinch of red pepper flakes

BROCCOLI

1 to 2 heads broccoli
  (see Note)
Juice of 1 lemon
Salt and freshly ground
  black pepper
¼ cup grated Pecorino
  Romano (optional)
½ to 1 cup toasted bread
  crumbs (optional)
¼ cup chopped fresh
  Italian parsley

*Note: Asparagus, cauliflower,
and carrots all make great
substitutions.*

Roasted Broccoli with Bagna Cauda, Pecorino, and Bread Crumbs

SERVES 2 TO 4

The bagna cauda is great on fish, beef, chicken, and as a salad dressing—and a little goes a long way! You can make larger batches of this sauce and refrigerate it for up to a week.

BAGNA CAUDA Combine anchovies, garlic, oil, cream, and butter in a food processor and process until smooth. Transfer mixture to a heavy-bottomed saucepan and cook over low heat for 15 minutes, stirring occasionally to prevent the sauce from separating.

Season with salt and red pepper flakes. Refrigerate until needed.

BROCCOLI Preheat oven to 450°F.

Separate the stalk from the head of broccoli. Trim stalk, peel stem, and slice diagonally into ¼-inch-thick slices. Cut head into 1-inch-thick slices. (The head will fall apart but the idea is that the floret pieces don't get too small after cooking.)

Place broccoli in a bowl, drizzle 2 to 3 tablespoons of bagna cauda over it, and toss. (It should be lightly coated.) Transfer to a baking sheet and roast for 15 minutes or until golden brown and crispy.

Put broccoli into a large bowl and add 2 tablespoons bagna cauda. Adjust seasoning with another 1 to 2 tablespoons, as desired. Season with a little lemon juice, salt, and pepper, to taste.

Serve on a platter and sprinkle with Pecorino Romano and bread crumbs, if using. Garnish with parsley.

¾ cup lukewarm water

1 package active dry yeast

2 cups high-gluten or
all-purpose flour, plus
extra for dusting

1 tsp granulated sugar

1 tsp salt, plus extra for
sprinkling

2 to 3 cups arugula leaves

1 Tbsp extra-virgin olive oil,
plus extra for brushing ·

Arugula Flatbread

SERVES 3 TO 4

The arugula in this recipe is mixed into the dough, creating a beautiful green-speckled flatbread that is fantastic straight out of the oven, or blistered over a gas stove top. Sprinkle it with salt, grated Parmesan, some fresh arugula and a squeeze of lemon, and you've got a great lunch or appetizer.

Combine water and yeast in a bowl and set aside for 5 minutes, until water turns cloudy and the yeast grows and bubbles.

In a food processor using the hook attachment, combine flour, sugar, salt, and arugula and mix well. (Alternatively, use your hands to mix.) Add yeast mixture and oil and blend until it forms a doughy ball.

Transfer dough to a floured surface and knead by hand for 5 minutes, or until smooth.

Coat a mixing bowl with oil and add dough, turning to coat. Cover bowl with plastic wrap and set aside at room temperature for 1 hour, or until dough has doubled in size. Punch the dough, which is ready for use. (Alternatively, cover dough in plastic wrap and store in the fridge overnight or the freezer for up to one month.)

Roll dough into baseball-sized rounds (2 to 3 ounces each). Using a rolling pin, roll dough into thin oblong shapes. Brush with olive oil and sprinkle with salt.

Preheat a grill to medium heat. Place flatbreads on grill and cook for 2 to 3 minutes, until puffed. Turn over and cook for another 2 to 3 minutes until golden brown. (Alternatively, place on an oiled baking sheet and bake at 350°F for 10 to 15 minutes.)

Cool slightly and serve.

Vendemmia Brian Clevenger

DON'T BE fooled by his baby-face—chef Brian Clevenger is on the fast-track to becoming a seasoned restaurateur. Born and raised in Anacortes, he left his roots to study cooking at a two-Michelin-star restaurant in Lyon, France, and the celebrated Delfina in San Francisco. With an affinity for refined foods, he then went to cook at both Tavolàta and Staple & Fancy.

But it was the business acumen he developed outside of the kitchen that helped him successfully open a string of restaurants at a time when Seattle was short of cooks. (In addition to Vendemmia, he owns two more pasta houses—Raccolto and Le Messe—and seafood market/specialty grocer East Anchor.) Like most chefs, Clevenger is infatuated with good products that taste great on their own, ones you don't have to mess with. And that's the beauty of marrying French technique and Italian food: by pairing exceptional

ingredients with a simple dish, you need to do very little to make it sing.

Vendemmia is a neighborhood trattoria on Madrona's main drag, serving simple and honest dishes to a receptive crowd. Neighbors can't get enough of his most basic dish: spaghetti with a simple red tomato sauce and fresh basil. (With a cooking method similar to risotto, it's labor intensive but so worth it.) This is what Clevenger is all about: uncomplicated food, quality ingredients, and repeat customers. Seattle is all the better for it.

→ Simple Spaghetti and
Tomato Sauce

TOMATO SAUCE

6 Tbsp extra-virgin olive oil

4 cloves garlic, crushed

1 tsp kosher salt, plus extra to taste

2 small white onions, finely chopped

1 (28-oz) can high-acid plum tomatoes

¼ cup fresh basil leaves

Freshly ground black pepper, to taste

1 tsp red pepper flakes, or to taste

PASTA

2 cups tomato sauce (see here)

1 lb dried spaghetti

2 Tbsp extra-virgin olive oil

¼ cup fresh basil leaves, plus extra for garnish

Kosher salt and freshly ground black pepper, to taste

Red pepper flakes, to taste

Simple Spaghetti and Tomato Sauce

SERVES 3 TO 4

Adding too much sauce to this dish will take away from the flavor of the pasta. Use just enough tomato sauce to coat the spaghetti.

TOMATO SAUCE In a nonreactive stockpot on medium heat, combine oil, garlic, and salt. Lightly cook the garlic. Remove and discard. Add onions and sauté for 4 minutes, or until translucent. Remove pot from heat.

Add tomatoes, including liquid, to the pot and cook on medium-high heat for 35 to 40 minutes, until tomatoes break down and sauce has thickened. Be sure to stir frequently with a wooden spoon, touching the bottom of the pan so the sauce doesn't burn. Pass the sauce through a food mill, then stir basil into it. Season with salt, pepper, and red pepper flakes to taste.

PASTA Pour tomato sauce into a large skillet.

Bring a large pot of salted water to boil. Add pasta and cook for 2 minutes, until it bends enough to fit in the skillet. Using tongs, transfer pasta to skillet, and then pour in 1½ cups of pasta water. Bring to a boil over medium heat, gently stir to agitate the pasta, and cook for 20 minutes, until the sauce thickens and the pasta is firm to the bite and not yet al dente. (Add more pasta water, if necessary.)

Stir in oil and basil leaves. Remove from heat. Season with salt, pepper, and red pepper flakes, to taste.

PLATING Divide the spaghetti into three to four bowls and garnish with basil. Serve immediately.

CHOCOLATE TERRINE

15 oz high-quality dark
   chocolate, 70% cacao
   (we prefer Valrhona),
   roughly chopped
5 bronze gelatin sheets
¼ cup granulated sugar
¼ cup cold water
5 egg whites
3 whole eggs
3 cups heavy cream
Unsalted butter, for
   greasing

Chocolate Terrine with Ganache and Fresh Berries

SERVES 8

CHOCOLATE TERRINE Bring a saucepan of water to a boil. Place chocolate in a heatproof bowl larger than the saucepan, and place on top. Stir until melted.

Put gelatin into a bowl of cold water and set aside for 10 minutes, until bloomed. Once it's bloomed, pull from the water and squeeze it dry.

Bring sugar and the ¼ cup cold water to a boil, add gelatin and remove from heat. Set aside to cool to room temperature. (Do not refrigerate: if you do, the gelatin will separate and rise to the top of your syrup.)

Meanwhile, in a mixer with a whisk attachment, combine egg yolks and whole eggs and whisk for 15 to 20 minutes, until they reach soft peaks. Add egg mixture to the cooled syrup and whisk until fully incorporated.

Pour mixture into bowl of melted chocolate and fold until fully incorporated.

Whip cream in a large bowl and fold into chocolate mixture until smooth (ensure there are no pockets of whipped cream).

Pour chocolate mixture into a lightly greased terrine pan. Using an offset spatula, level mixture and cool in the refrigerator overnight to set.

CONTINUED OVERLEAF

CHOCOLATE GANACHE

10 oz high-quality dark
  chocolate, 70% cacao,
  roughly chopped
2 cups heavy cream
Fresh seasonal berries,
  for garnish

CHOCOLATE GANACHE Bring a saucepan of water to a boil. Place chocolate in a heatproof bowl larger than the saucepan, and place on top. Stir until melted.

In a separate saucepan, bring cream to a simmer over medium heat. Pour cream into melted chocolate and mix well.

ASSEMBLY Unmold the terrine from the pan onto a cutting board so it's easy to portion. Pour enough ganache over the terrine to fully cover it and set aside for 2 hours to set. (Depending on the size of your terrine mold, you may have some left over.)

Place a slice of terrine on each individual plate. Garnish with berries and serve.

Metric Conversion Chart

VOLUME

Imperial or U.S.	Metric
⅛ tsp	0.5 ml
¼ tsp	1 ml
½ tsp	2.5 ml
¾ tsp	4 ml
1 tsp	5 ml
½ Tbsp	8 ml
1 Tbsp	15 ml
1½ Tbsp	23 ml
2 Tbsp	30 ml
¼ cup	60 ml
⅓ cup	80 ml
½ cup	125 ml
⅔ cup	165 ml
¾ cup	185 ml
1 cup	250 ml
1¼ cups	310 ml
1⅓ cups	330 ml
1½ cups	375 ml
1⅔ cups	415 ml
1¾ cups	435 ml
2 cups	500 ml
2¼ cups	560 ml
2⅓ cups	580 ml
2½ cups	625 ml
2¾ cups	690 ml
3 cups	750 ml
4 cups/1 qt	1 L
5 cups	1.25 L
6 cups	1.5 L
7 cups	1.75 L
8 cups/2 qts	2 L

WEIGHT

Imperial or U.S.	Metric
½ oz	15 g
1 oz	30 g
2 oz	60 g
3 oz	85 g
4 oz (¼ lb)	115 g
5 oz	140 g
6 oz	170 g
7 oz	200 g
8 oz (½ lb)	225 g
9 oz	255 g
10 oz	285 g
11 oz	310 g
12 oz (¾ lb)	340 g
13 oz	370 g
14 oz	400 g
15 oz	425 g
16 oz (1 lb)	450 g
1¼ lbs	570 g
1½ lbs	670 g
2 lbs	900 g
3 lbs	1.4 kg
4 lbs	1.8 kg
5 lbs	2.3 kg
6 lbs	2.7 kg

LIQUID MEASURES
(for alcohol)

Imperial or U.S.	Metric
1 fl oz	30 ml
2 fl oz	60 ml
3 fl oz	90 ml
4 fl oz	120 ml

CANS AND JARS

Imperial or U.S.	Metric
14 oz	398 ml
28 oz	796 ml

LINEAR

Imperial or U.S.	Metric
⅛ inch	3 mm
¼ inch	6 mm
½ inch	12 mm
¾ inch	2 cm
1 inch	2.5 cm
1¼ inches	3 cm
1½ inches	3.5 cm
1¾ inches	4.5 cm
2 inches	5 cm
2½ inches	6.5 cm
3 inches	7.5 cm
4 inches	10 cm
5 inches	12.5 cm
6 inches	15 cm
7 inches	18 cm
8 inches	20 cm
9 inche	23 cm
10 inches	25 cm
11 inches	28 cm
12 inches (1 foot)	30 cm
13 inches	33 cm
18 inches	46 cm

TEMPERATURE
(for oven temperatures, see chart below)

Imperial or U.S.	Metric
90°F	32°C
120°F	49°C
125°F	52°C
130°F	54°C
135°F	57°C
140°F	60°C
145°F	63°C
150°F	66°C
155°F	68°C
160°F	71°C
165°F	74°C
170°F	77°C
175°F	80°C
180°F	82°C
185°F	85°C
190°F	88°C
195°F	91°C
200°F	93°C
225°F	107°C
250°F	121°C
275°F	135°C
300°F	149°C
325°F	163°C
350°F	177°C
360°F	182°C
375°F	191°C

OVEN TEMPERATURE

Imperial or U.S.	Metric
200°F	95°C
250°F	120°C
275°F	135°C
300°F	150°C
325°F	160°C
350°F	180°C
375°F	190°C
400°F	200°C
425°F	220°C
450°F	230°C

BAKING PANS

Imperial or U.S.	Metric
9- × 5-inch loaf pan	2 L loaf pan
18- × 13-inch baking sheet	46 × 33 cm baking sheet

Acknowledgments

I am so incredibly grateful to the many people who helped me accomplish a project that seemed, at times, overwhelming. Without them, none of this would have happened.

First, thank you to the team at Figure 1, especially Michelle Meade for being not just my editor but a cheerleader, mentor, and, ultimately, a friend. I'd like to extend my gratitude to Danielle Centoni, writer and author of *Portland Cooks*, who was an important resource during the early stages.

Thank you to my team of recipe testers—Anu Elford, Justin Khanna, Katie Okumura, Melissa Peterman, Tiffany Ran, Denise Sakaki—who worked tirelessly around the clock to ensure the recipes were bookworthy. A special thank you to my mother, LeAnn Perry, for her contribution and for greatly inspiring my love of all things food.

The photography dream team brought the recipes and stories to life. The immensely talented photographer Charity Burggraaf has a meticulous eye for detail, Renée Beaudoin beautified the shots with her food styling and props, Audrey Kelly helped the photo shoot run smoothly, and art director Naomi MacDougall led with a clear vision. It was truly one of my favorite aspects of this project. Thank you to local artist Natasha Alphonse for the beautiful handcrafted ceramics.

Above all, thank you to all the chefs and bartenders in this book who trusted me with telling their stories. There is not enough space on this page to fully express my appreciation of your talents and your time. It was a dream come true to collaborate with some of the most inspired people I have ever had the pleasure of knowing and meeting. You were patient, generous, and accommodating throughout the entire process. Seattle is one of the best food cities in the country because of all of you, and I could not be any prouder of this book we have accomplished as a team.

Index

Page numbers in italics refer to photos.

About the Author

JULIEN PERRY has been a food and lifestyle writer and editor for more than twenty years, and has worked as a food editor for *Seattle Weekly*, *Seattle Business Magazine*, *Eater Seattle*, and *Seattle Magazine*. Her work has also been featured in *Food & Wine* and on the Food Network. An alumnus of Seattle Art Institute's Baking and Pastry program, she cofounded the One Night Only Project—a roving dinner series that partners with the city's food and beverage powerhouses—and Chefodex, a chef-for-hire service featuring a roster of Seattle's foremost culinary talent.